A PRETTY KETTLE OF FISH

Brian Waters

Pen Press Publishers Ltd

First published in Great Britain by
Pen Press Publishers Ltd
25 Eastern PLace
Brighton
BN2 1GJ

ISBN13: 978-1-905621-69-9

Printed and bound in the UK

A catalogue record of this book is available from
the British Library

Cover design by Jacqueline Abromeit

Introduction

Is there anywhere on earth where fish does not come into daily life in one way or another? We boil, steam, fry, smoke, bake, poach, salt, curry, and pickle them. We have them in sunflower, vegetable, and olive oils and with a multitude of sauces and marinades, we have them in pies and covered in breadcrumbs, we even eat them raw. And we batter them and eat their fingers, and the oils from their body give us health and vitality.

Great poets like Tennyson, De la Mare, and Sir Walter Scott have written poetry about them, and Edward Lear wrote a lot of nonsense about them. The film industry have made movies of them from the great white shark (Jaws) to the smallest clown fish (Nimo) and told stories of the brave and gallant deep sea fisherman (The Perfect Storm). Deep sea fishermen are ranked forth in the top ten most dangerous jobs.

They come in more colours than there are in a rainbow, and the most troubled mind can find peace and solace just watching them swimming around in our ponds and aquariums.

They give us sport in our rivers, lakes, and out on the ocean blue. The old and the young, the able and the disabled, the rich and the poor can all enjoy the sport on equal terms, and race, creed and colour are all forgotten when out fishing. Your status in life may be a humble one and your fishing gear may consist of a crooked branch, a piece of string, and a bent pin, and yet you might, just might catch a record breaking monster of a fish and you will be exalted by your fellow fisherman and your name will be written forever more in the record books.

We owe friend fish a great debt of gratitude and yet we treat this most valuable friend badly; we pollute rivers, lakes, and oceans – their homes! We take from them more than they can give us and many of them – more friend to us than us to them – are now on the verge of extinction. Should we lose just one species we will be the greatest losers; we should enjoy the sport they give us, the food they give us, and the health they give us, but not ask of them more than they can give. For many of them the time has come to ask not what friend fish can do for us but what we can do for friend fish.

Brian Stephen Waters

An Apology

Many of the entries in this book were submitted to me by fishermen themselves, unfortunately many of them did not know who the author was.

I have made every possible effort to make contact with copyright owners; those who have granted permission to use their work have my grateful thanks.

To those who I have not been able to contact I hope you will forgive me for taking your permission for granted. I also invite you to write to the publishers so as your work will be given full acknowledgement in any further editions of this book.

Saint Andrew

Saint Andrew is the patron saint of fishermen and anglers.

Andrew was born in Bethsaida
and was crucified on a saltire
(an X shaped cross).

The fishing net is the emblem of St Andrew,
recalling his vocation before he was summoned by Jesus
to be a 'Fisher of men'.

His name means: 'Strong … Manly'

His feast day is celebrated on November 30th.

KETTLE

The word Kettle is a corruption of Kiddle which is a barrier in a river with an opening fitted with nets to catch fish. How the expression 'A pretty kettle of fish' came to mean an 'awkward state of affairs' is not known. However, legend has it that when a fisherman returned to his kiddle or kettle to check his catch, and found only flotsam, it was said; all he had was a pretty kiddle/kettle of fish.

* * *

A Fisherman's Prayer

Grant me grace, O Lord,
To catch a fish so large
That even I,
In boasting of it afterward,
Shall have no need to lie.

* * *.

NONSENSE RHYME

Brian Stephen Waters
1942 - ....

I Saw

I saw a fishwife making bread
I saw a dragon fish with a fiery head
I saw a starfish in a square
I saw an angel fish in the air
I saw a dogfish walk a mile
I saw a clownfish with a smile
I saw a pearl fish in a box
I saw a cowfish marry an ox
I saw a goldfish made of steel
I saw a swordfish dance a reel
I saw a lantern fish light up the sky
I saw a goosefish in a pie
I saw a flying fish fly away
I saw a cardinal fish kneel to pray
I saw a catfish kiss a dog
I saw a parrotfish mixing grog
I saw a fisherman who saw these too
And he will confirm what I tell you

THE FISH COMES LAST

Our vernal signs the Ram begins

Then comes the Bull, in May the Twins;

The Crab in June, next Leo shines

And Virgo ends the northern signs.

The balance brings Autumnal fruits,

The Scorpion stings, the Archer shoots;

December's goat brings wintry blast,

Aquarius rain, the Fish comes last.

EEL

Anguilla Anguilla

The freshwater eel is rated a sporting proposition by fishermen when it has grown considerably. Eels migrating to the sea weigh one and a half to three pounds are quite common, but specialists are more interested in catching the larger, non-migrating eel of four pounds plus. This is a summer and autumn pursuit in lakes and canals.

Method: Free lining and legering

Baits: Small dead fish

Night sessions best. Carp-strength tackle and wire traces essential.

Status – Numerous

* * *

For centuries European eels had mystified fishermen because young eels (elvers) could never be found. In the early nineteen hundreds scientists discovered that the eels lay their eggs far from Europe in the warm waters of the Sargasso sea. After hatching, the young eels start their 3,000 mile, three-year journey to Europe. On reaching their destination the male remains at the mouth of the rivers while the females will swim far upstream; sometimes leaving the rivers to slither through wet grass to reach preferred ponds and lakes. They remain in the rivers, ponds and lakes for several years until they are mature. They then set off on the return journey back to the Sargasso sea to spawn and die.

The eel can go without food for up to four years.

A female European eel was 88 years old when she died in Halsingborg, Sweden in 1948. She was the oldest fish ever recorded.

5

SONG OF THE HATED EEL
Arthur Guiterman

(1871–1934)

Ho, the slimy, squirmy, slithery eel!
He swallows your hook with malignant zeal
He tangles your line and he gums your reel
The slimy, squirmy, slithery eel.

Ho, the slimy, squirmy, slithery eel
He cannot be held in a grip of steel,
And when he is dead he is hard to peel
The slimy, squirmy, slithery eel.

Ho, the slimy, squirmy, slithery eel
The sorriest catch in an angler's creel
Who said he was fit for a Christian meal
The slimy, squirmy, slithery eel.

Ho, the slimy, squirmy, slithery eel
Malevolent Serpent! Who does reveal
What eloquent fisherman say and feel
Concerning the slithery, slimy eel?

FLY FISHING
Samuel Johnson
1709-1784

*

* Fly *

Fishing may be

A very pleasant

Amusement; but angling

Or float fishing I

Can only compare

To a stick with

A worm at

One

End

And

A

Fool

At the other

FISHING TRAWLERS

Some fishing trawlers are big enough to hold a dozen 747 jumbo jets.

These massive ships use light aircraft to locate the vast shoals of fish

from the air.

It is estimated that a quarter of every fishing net trawled contains fish that are: A. too small; B. the wrong type; C. caught in the wrong season.

All these unwanted fish are dumped back into the ocean … mostly dead.

It is believed that as much as 22 million tonnes of unwanted fish are dumped back into the sea every year.

It is estimated that over 40 million tonnes of fish are caught each year. This is only a small fraction (perhaps only five per cent) of the total population of food fish in the sea.

There are over 30,000 species of fish discovered so far.

About a thousand species are thought to be endangered. Most of them are freshwater species that have been harmed by pollution or over fishing. There may however be many more at risk.

* * *

For every kilogram of shrimp taken from the sea, about four kilograms of fish and other marine life is destroyed.

* * *

A shrimp's heart is in its head.

NONSENSE TALES

Brian Stephen Waters

1942 - ....

The Man Who Wasn't There

Once upon a time three fishermen set out for a day's fishing. Two of the fishermen were naked and the other had no clothes on. They had three rods: two had no hooks and the other had no line. They set out before daylight and went far, far, far away. Then they went still farther.

They came to a river where they caught three salmon. They missed two of them and the other one got away. The fisherman who had no clothes on put the salmon that got away in his pocket.

"My goodness," said the fishermen, "how are we going to cook the salmon that got away?"

The three fishermen then went on their way. They went far, far, and still farther. At last they came to a house that had neither walls, nor roof, nor door, nor windows. The three fishermen struck three great blows on the door that wasn't there: Pam! Pam! Pam!

The man who wasn't there answered, "What do you want? What do you want?"

"Would you do us a good turn?" asked the fisherman, "Will you lend us your pot, so we can cook the salmon that got away from us?"

"Good heavens, sirs!" the man replied, "we have only three pots. Two of them are leaking and the other has a hole in it."

* * *

Everybody, Somebody, Anybody and Nobody

This is the story of four fishermen. Their names were everybody, somebody, anybody and nobody. There was a very important fishing tournament coming up that had to be organised, and everybody was sure that somebody would do it. Anybody could have done it, but nobody did it. Somebody got angry about that, because it was everybody's job. Everybody thought anybody could do it, but nobody realized that everybody wouldn't do it. It all ended up with everybody blaming somebody when nobody did what anybody could have done.

STURGEON

Acipenser Oxyrhychus

The statute **PEROGATIVA REGIS** (of the King's/Queen's Perogative) dates back to the reign of Edward II (1284–1327), in which the law states that "The Monarch shall have throughout his realm any great sturgeons taken from the sea or elsewhere within his realm." It meant that all sturgeons were the property of the monarch and could not be disposed of without the monarch's consent.

In 1970 the Queen agreed to allow her prerogative right to the great sturgeon to be abolished. The Law Commission recommended a change to the law to parliament. The proposed change was defeated by the House of Lords in 1971. It means that the Queen still has rights to the great sturgeon taken from the seas and rivers in and around Britain.

Status – Critically endangered,
close to extinction in some part of its range

* * *

MISSISSIPPI PADDLEFISH

Polyodon Spatiliulia

The Mississippi Paddlefish is also called the Spoonbill Catfish, although it is no relation to the catfish family. It is, in fact, a close relative of the sturgeon and like its illustrious cousin it produces high quality caviar. But unlike the sturgeon, whose caviar is black, the paddlefish caviar is green.

Status – At Risk

COD - NUNDRUMS

*
* It *

Counts

Your of size

How not that

The it's

It's

Use

Your rod

*
* If *

Trouble

Neither mouths

Keep are get

Their men

Would

Fish

Like

They

Shut into

Answers page 148

SILLY FISH

Which fish go to heaven when they die?
Angel fish.

*

What is the best way to communicate with a fish?
Drop it a line.

*

Which part of a fish weighs the most?
The scales.

*

Where do fish wash?
In a river basin.

*

What kind of a horse can swim under water?
A seahorse.

*

Where do fish keep their money?
In a river bank.

*

What's the difference between a fish and a piano?
You can't tuna fish.

*

Why was the carp hiding in the pond weed?
It was just being Koi.

*

Which sea creature eats its victims two by two?
Noah's shark!

*

What did the fish say when it hit a concrete wall?
Dam!

*

Which fish can perform operations?
A surgeonfish.

*

Stop shouting you're giving me a
Head-hake!

*

You'll have to speak up I'm hard of
Herring.

*

I didn't go to work today I told the boss I was
Eel!

*

THE TIDAL THAMES

Up to forty boats once worked between Wandsworth and Hammersmith, taking up to 50,000 smelt a day. Salmon, whitebait, shad, flounders and eel were also plentiful. Each year over a million lamperns were sold to Dutch fishermen for bait. But by 1960 the tidal Thames was declared dead of all fish. A gigantic scheme was begun to extend London's major sewage system to improve the quality of the water of the tidal Thames, and today the tidal Thames is internationally recognised as a leading example of a successful clean-up campaign. The tidal Thames now supports over 119 species of fish. They include:

FRESHWATER
Bream, carp, dace,
Pike, perch, roach

HURYHALINE*
Bass, eel, flounder,
Salmon, trout, shad

MARINE
Dab, herring, sprat
Sole, mullet, rockling

* Fish that can live in both fresh and salt water.

A school of fish
A pack of perch
A pod of whiting
A run of salmon
A shoal of pilchards
A troupe of dogfish
A lap of cod
A hive of oysters
A bundle of rays
A flutter of jellyfish

A fall of spawn
A grind of blackfish
A draught of eels
A brace of pike
A quantity of smelt
A hover of trout
A bed of mackerel
A glean of herring
A drift of anglers
A flight of hooks

Exaggeration of fishermen

PERICLES

Third Fisherman:
"Master, I marvel how the fishes live in the sea."
First Fisherman:
"Why, as men do a-land, the great ones eat up the little
ones."

Pericles, Act 1 Scene 1

* * *

ANTONY AND CLEOPATRA

Give me mine angel; we'll do th' river;
There – my music playing far off – I will
Betray tawny finned fishes; my bended
Hook shall piece their slimy jaws; and,
I shall draw them up, I'll think them
Every one an Antony and say "Ha, Ha, you're caught."

Antony and Cleopatra, Act 2 Scene 5

The Fastest Fish

Maximum Recorded Speed

	km/h	mph
Sailfish	122	69
Marlin	80	50
Wahoo	77	48
Bluefin Tuna	76	47
Yellowfin Tuna	74	46
Blue Shark	69	43
Bone Fish	64	40
Swordfish	109	68
Tarpon	56	35
Tiger Shark	53	33

There are many sharks that could qualify for a place in the above list, but this would cause the list to become "shark infested" so they are not included.

A Tarpon swimming at maximum speed has been known to leap eighteen feet (5 metres) high and make a thirty feet (9 metres) arc.

CAT SHARK

Cephaloslyllium Ventriosum

The cat shark is also known as the "Swell Shark" because of its ability to take in vast amounts of air or water when threatened. When filled with air, they have been known to float for several days before expelling the air from their bodies.

Status – Not Threatened

* * *

BLUEFISH

Pomatomus Saltatrix

Bluefish are the most voracious carnivores of all marine fish. It is estimated that as many as 1,000,000,000 live off the Atlantic coast of the United States. Each bluefish will eat as many as ten other fish a day, so 1,000,000,000 bluefish will eat 10,000,000,000 each day. They kill more fish than they can eat. When attacking shoals of herring or mackerel they will bite larger fish in two leaving half to float away before going on to attack the next fish.

Bluefish probably kill over 2,000,000,000,000 other fish in a year; most about their own size. The average weight of a bluefish is between 3 and 5lbs. Their peak weight is around 30lbs. The record weight is 31lbs plus. They can grow up to three feet long and can live for about eleven years.

Status – Numerous

PIKE

Esox Lucius

Widespread in Britain and Ireland, this ferocious predator swims waters great and small. Lean built and large of mouth, it is a fast-moving hunter of small fish. A 20 pounder is an excellent catch, but the species is reputed to grow upward of 60lb in Scottish lochs, notably Loch Lomond.

Methods: Float fishing, legering, freelining, spinning etc. Baits: Live and dead fish, especially herring.

Status – Not Threatened

*

An angler fishing on one of Canada's many lakes hooked an enormous pike. After a long struggle he landed the giant fish. Unhooking the monster he laid it on the bank next to his shotgun. The feisty fish began to thrash and flap around knocking over the shotgun; the gun went off killing the fisherman outright.

*

When Christ was crucified it was said that all the fishes dived under the water in terror except the pike who lifted its head above the water and witnessed the whole crucifixion.

On the head of the pike can be seen marks that resemble the cross – three nails and a sword.

I OFTEN SIT

*
* I *
Often sit
And think
And fish and sit
And fish and think
And sit and
Fish and
Think and
Wish
That
I could
Get a drink!

YOU CAN HAVE

*
* You *
Can Have
Fried Fish
Fresh, Fish Fried
Fresh, Fresh
Fried Fish
Fresh
Fish
Fried,
Or
Fish Fresh Fried

NURSERY RHYME

One, two, three, four, five
Once I caught a fish alive.
Why did you let him go?
Because he bit my finger so.
Six, seven, eight, nine, ten
Shall we go to fish again?
Not today some other time
For I have broke my fishing line.

Terence McDiddler
The three fingered fiddler
Can, if you please, charm
The fish from the seas.

Brenda Blonkin braised a box of British bloaters,
A box of British bloaters Brenda Blonkin braised.
If Brenda Blonkin braised a box of British bloaters,
Where is the box of British bloaters Brenda Blonkin
braised?

NIGEL

"I didn't see you in church on Sunday,
Nigel,
I hear you were playing football."
"That's not the truth,
Vicar,
and I have the fish to prove it."

THE POLICEMAN

A motorist was ranting and raving at a policeman
After being stopped for speeding.
He was pointing angrily at the passing cars that were going
Much faster than he had been.
The policeman asked the motorist,
"Do you ever go fishing, sir?"
The motorist, a keen angler, smiles and replies,
"Yes," thinking he had found a kindred spirit.
"Never catch them all… do we, sir?"
Asks the policeman.

PEARLFISH

Echiodon Drummondi

The twelve inch (30cm) Pearlfish is also known as the sea cucumber fish. But the Pearlfish does not live up to its beautiful name. To protect itself from predators it lives in the anus of the sea-cucumber, and uses its host as a lair to catch its food. Its own anus is located near its throat so only the head of the Pearlfish will leave the host when nature calls. Pearlfish pair for life living inside the sea-cucumber.

Status – Threatened

* * *

STOUT INFANTFISH

Schindleria Brevipinguis

The stout infantfish is the smallest and lightest fish in the world. They are so small and light it would take a million of them to weigh one kilogram. Mature males are just seven millimetres in length. The largest infantfish to date is a female measuring 8.4mm long. The previous holder of the record for world's smallest fish was the dwarf goby (Trimmatom Nanus). The dwarf goby has an average length of 8.6mm for males and 8.9mm for females. The stout infantfish belongs to the family Schinleriidae, of which the dwarf goby is a member. The stout infantfish may be the most abundant coral reef fish in the world. They reach maturity between twenty and sixty days. They spawn only once in their lives – laying between 12 and 15 eggs, after which they die.

Status – Data Deficient

To A Fish
Leigh Hunt
1784-1859

You strange, astonished-looking, angle-faced, dreary-mouthed,
   Gaping wretches of the sea gulping salt everlastingly
Cold-blooded, though with red your blood be graced,
   And mute, though dwellers in the roaring waste;
     And you, all shapes beside, that fishy be –
Some round, some flat, some long, all devilry,
     Legless, unloving, infamously chaste;

    O scaly, slippery, wet, swift, staring wights*
What isn't ye do? What life load? Eh, dull goggles?
    How do ye vary your vile days and nights?
How pass your Sundays? Are ye still but joggles
In ceaseless wash? Still nought but gape and bites,
And drinks, and stares, diversified with hoggles?

                            * creatures

A Fish Answers

Amazing monster! That for aught I know,
With the first sight of thee didst make our race
Forever stare! O flat and shocking face,
Grimly divided from the breast below!

Thou that on dry land horribly dost go
With a split body and most ridiculous pace,
Prong after prong, disgracer of all grace,
Long-useless-finned, haired, upright, unwet, slow!

O breather of unbreathable, sword-sharp air,
How canst exist? How bear thyself, thou dry
And dreary sloth? What particle canst share
Of the only blessed life, the watery?

I sometimes see of ye an actual pair
Go by! Linked fin by fin! Most odiously.

The Name To Go With The Job

Cecil Fin
President of the Scottish Fishermen's Federation.

A Carp
Head of the National Fish Marketing Board in the Netherlands.

Steve Haddock
Scientist at the Monterey Bay Aquarium Research Institute.

William Dolphin
Expert in marine sonar in Boston University.

* * *

Fish in Symbolism
The fish is the symbol for freedom from all restraint.

ROACH
Trustworthy – Reliable

CARP
Courage – Virility

EEL
Deviousness – Fertility

SALMON
Courage – Wisdom

SEAHORSE
Confidence – Grace

SHARK
Survival – Adaptability

MACKEREL

Scomber Scombrus

Mackerel swarm inshore around the British coastline during the warm months and is easily caught as food and as bait for the larger game on multi-hook feather rigs fished sink-and-draw from boat and shore.

Sporting techniques include light tackle spinning and fly fishing with trout tackle.

Shoal mackerel average about 1lb. Bigger individuals (4lb plus), are occasionally hooked on bottom baits from deep water marks.

Status – Threatened

* * *

PROVERBS

You
lay
a
sprat
to
catch
a
mackerel.

Though you are hungry
it is better to have a
mackerel tomorrow
than a sprat today

MACKEREL

Mackerel can shoal in countless millions. One ship was reported to have steamed round a shoal 50 miles in circumference, and that was just one shoal of many on the move in the North Sea at the time.

A great grampus dolphin, of the type that follows the massive shoals, was once seen to be struggling for life when it ventured too far into one of these massive shoals. The sheer mass and weight of the racing mackerel was preventing the dolphin rising to the surface to breathe.

Other predators such as the toothed whales swim in circles beneath the great shoals releasing air bubbles to force the mackerel into tight balls. They then race upward breaking the surface taking thousands of fish in one gulp

Bad Day At The River

E. U RIEU

1885-1972

The overlord of roaches
Has made a royal rule,
For roach and rudd and loaches
And fish from pond and pool.
Proclaimed it in the river,
And nailed it to a tree;
That no fish whatsoever
Is to be caught by me.

Signed by the king of roaches
In this his royal stream;
Sealed by the lord of loaches;
Attested by a bream;
Engrossed by twenty perches;
Translated into French;
Read out in all the churches
And broadcast by a tench.

* * *

The Fisherman's Ring

A seal ring, with which the Pope is invested at his election, bears the heraldic design of St Peter fishing from a boat. It is used for sealing papal briefs and is broken up at the Pope's death by the chamberlain of the Roman church.

* * *

Loaves and Fishes

O Lord, who made the loaves and fishes,
Look down upon these two dishes
And, though they be exceedingly small,
Make them enough, we pray, for all;
For if they all our stomachs fill,
Heaven will have wrought a miracle.

* * *

St Peter and the Haddock

According to tradition it was the haddock in whose mouth St Peter found a stater (a piece of money). The two marks on the fish's neck are said to be the impression of St Peter's finger and thumb.

I.K.TH.U.S

IESOUS	KRISTO	THEOU	UIOS	SOTOR
I	K	TH	U	S
Jesus	Christ	Son Of	God	Saviour

The Greek word for fish is:

IKTHUS

* * *

Christian Symbols

It was with the symbol of the fish
that the early Christians identified
themselves to each other.

Three fish in a circle nose to tail represent

The Holy Trinity

Father, Son and Holy Ghost

A list of prices to be charged at Billingsgate fish market in the reign of Edward I (1272–1307)

	Shillings	Pence
	S	d
Best Plaice	0	½
A dozen Best Soles	3	0
Best Cod or Ling	3	0
Best Haddock	2	0
Best Mullet	2	0
Best Dorac or John Dory	5	0
Best Conger	10	0
Best Turbot	6	0
Best Mackerel in Lent	1	0
Best Mackerel out of Lent	0	½
Best Gurnard	1	0
Best Merlin (Whiting) for four	1	0
Best Thames or Severn Lamprey	4	0
Best fresh Oysters, a gallon	2	0
Best sea-hog (porpoise)	6	8
Best fresh Salmon from Christmas to Easter, four for	5	0
Best roach in summer	1	0

AESOP'S FABLES

A fisherman was hauling in his net which he had cast a short while before. It was full of fish large and small; but the little ones escaped through the meshes and got back into the water while the larger were gathered up and emptied into the boat.

Moral: Safety often lies in insignificance.

* * *

There was a fisherman who was also a skilled flautist. One day he went down with his flute and nets to the seashore, where, standing on a ledge of rock, he began playing a tune thinking that the fish would be attracted by the sweet sound of his instrument. He wasted a good deal of his time in this way, and then, finding his hopes disappointed, he threw away his flute, took up his net, made a cast, and hauled in a splendid catch. He shook out the fish, and said, as he saw them leaping on the beach: "Ha! You brutes, you wouldn't dance when I played, and now when I stop you do just that."

The fable is addressed to those who do everything at the wrong time.

PLEASANT PLAICE

*
* A *
pleasant
place to place
a plaice is in a
place where
the
plaice
are
pleased
to be placed

A SELFISH SHELLFISH

*
* A *
selfish
shellfish
Smelt a stale
Fish, if the
Stale fish
was a
smelt
the
selfish
shellfish
smelt a smelt

Nile Perch

Lates Niloticus

The fish that once was a god.

When thinking of big game fish, fishermen's minds turn to the giants of the oceans. But this freshwater colossus can exceed over three hundred pounds; rightfully taking its place alongside the ocean giants such as the marlin, blue fin tuna etc. Should you do battle with this giant you are advised to take along the heaviest and best tackle there is, as nothing less will do.

Two thousand years ago an Egyptian cult on the upper Nile worshipped the Nile perch as a god, naming the city of Latpolis (Esneh) in its honour. On death it was mummified and given a preferential position among the other animal "gods" once exalted by the ancient Egyptians.

Today, game fishermen still consider the Nile perch to be an adversary of the highest order.

Status – Data Deficient

* * *

PERCH

Perca Fluviatilis

Bold vertical stripes and spiny leading dorsal fin distinguish the perch. This common fish of lakes and rivers is big at 2lb, and, at 4lb plus the catch of a lifetime.

Methods: Spinning, float, paternoster, running leger.

Baits: Small fish, worm maggot.

Lake perch feed at all levels, hunting near weed and reed beds during mild periods. In winter they seek deep water. River perch inhabit slacks and backwaters.

Status – Vulnerable

Two Parrots

*

* Two *

Parrots

sitting on a perch

One parrot said to

the other

parrot

"Do

you
smell fish?"

Sea Sick Fish

Sailing through the Mediterranean, scientists proved that fish can become sea-sick. Kept in tanks aboard ship, fish weighing from two to seventy pounds became just as sick as any passenger or crew member when sailing through choppy seas.

Eaten Up By Worms or Fishes

*

* Buried *
in the earth
Or drowned in
the main, eaten up
by worms or fishes,
I pray the
pious may
obtain
for
happy
times
their wishes.

Not So Pea-Brained

Scientists have found that fish are not as pea-brained as
once thought. They have revealed that fish can complete
complex mental tasks that would baffle more intelligent
animals such as dogs and can remember these tasks months
later proving they are not the numb sculls who can't
remember things for more than a few seconds. Boffins also
proved that fish recognise their owners and will go into a
sulk if someone other than their owners feed them.

A Young Fellow Named Fisher

*

*There *
was a young
fellow named
Fisher, who was fishing
for fish in a fissure;
A cod with a grin
pulled the fisher-
man in now
they're
fishing
the fissure for Fisher.

Field of Fishes

*

* Once *
a fisher met a
Fisher in a field
of fishes, said a fisher
to a Fisher can
a Fisher
tell
a
fisher
where
a Fisher fishes?

Phobias That Could Ruin A Fisherman's life

Fish	Icthyophobia
Moon	Selenophobia
Night	Noctiphobia
Ocean/Sea	Thalassophobia
Rain	Ombrophobia
Rivers	Potomophobia
Solitude	Monophobia
Waiting	Macrophobia
Water	Hydrophobia
Waves	Cymophobia
Worms	Scoleciphobia

Queen of the Bloaters
Thomas Hood
1799-1854

If you were queen of bloaters
And I was king of soles,
The sea we'd wag our fins in
Nor heed the crooked pins in.
The water dropped by boaters
To catch our headless joles;
If you were queen of bloaters
And I was king of soles.

* * *

Starve Her Joe

Starve her, starve her,
Starve her, Joe –
If she has a bloater
Pinch the roe, roe, roe!
Bet your mother-in-law
Will go if you only starve her, Joe.

* * *

Fishie Fishie

Fishie, fishie, in the brook,
Daddy catch him with a hook,
Mama fry him in a pan,
Johnny eat him like a man

The Fishmonger

Walter de la Mare
1873-1956

In June it must be very nice
To bask about a block of ice –
And watch the world go broiling by
Under a hot and windless sky;
Then turn aside, and, sniffing see
Perennial mounds of shrimps for tea;
How genial, too, when fancying dab,
To slip one from one's marble slab;
Or, when the stars begin to twinkle,
To broach an unofficial winkle;
Or to descend in morning slipper
And not to have to buy a kipper.
This must be very pleasant, and
As pleasant too, to, understand,
When you have cod – are dining off it –
You're only eating so much profit.
Solacing thoughts like these must stir
The musings of a fishmonger.

Babby Battering

Cyril Fletcher
1913-2005

This is the tale of Bluebell Bishop
Who kept a nice fried chip and fishop.
As well as her husband Bert who worked,
She'd also a small son who irked.
Cos he made such an infernal noise
Whilst upstairs playing with his toys.
So much against their dearest wish,
He was brought downstairs among the fish
He paired the kippers from those odd size,
And he played marbles with the cods' eyes.
His mother cried: "You've gone too far …
Take your water-pistol out of the vin-e-gar."

But whist Mum and Dad were busy cooking
He had no time to keep on looking
And so it was in all that clatter
The boy fell in the pan of batter.
And though he kicked and booed and cried,
With hake and cod was nicely fried.
Then in the general rush and fuss
Was sold with chips as octopus.
It was not until the shop was cleared
They'd found their son had disappeared,
And though they sought him high and low,
And even down the overflow,
There was no trace of little Bill
Except the profit in the till.

HALIBUT

Hippoglossus Hippoglossus

Rarely caught on rod or line, the giant halibut of the cold northerly waters above Scotland offers a unique target for big game anglers. Stout gear is absolutely essential as this jumbo flat fish frequently weighs between 50lb and several hundred pounds.

Tackle: Heavy duty boat rod 50lb minimum 10.0 hook.
Method: Whole fish bait drifted across the same rocky grounds fished by commercial halibut long-liners.

Shoals of halibut once swam in countless numbers off the coast of New England. Fishing boats could land as much as 20,000 pounds of halibut a day. Through over-fishing halibut is now almost extinct off the coast of north west America.

Status – Highly Threatened

* * *

WEATHER FISH

Migurnus Fossillis

Long before the weather was forecast to us by newspapers, radio and television, people relied on signs to tell them what the weather would be. A red sky at night would indicate a fine day tomorrow, but a red sky in the morning would indicate a bad day ahead. Cows sitting down meant inclement weather was on its way.

For a time across Europe, people kept the weather fish in ponds and wells as a living barometer. It was believed that the weather fish could predict stormy weather twenty-four hours in advance. This ordinary little fish is so sensitive to atmospheric pressure that a drop in pressure that precedes a storm would cause the fish to become nervous and agitated, swimming rapidly around the pond or well. This agitated restlessness was believed by the fishes' keepers to be the onset of bad weather.

Status – Not Threatened

* * *

A Duck

Leo Tolstoy
1828-1910

A duck was swimming along a river looking for fish. The whole day passed without her finding a single fish. When the night came she saw the moon reflected on the water, and thinking it was a fish, she dived down to catch it. The other ducks saw her and they all made fun of her.

From that day the duck was so ashamed and so timid, that even when she did see a fish under water she would not try to catch it.

And before long she died of hunger.

A CURE FOR TUBERCULOSIS

*
* The *
laying of a
dead fish on
the chest of a
patient was
thought
to
help
cure
tuberculosis.

* * *

TEACH A MAN TO FISH

*
* You *
can give a
man a fish and
he will eat for a
day, you can
teach a man
to fish and
he will
eat
for
a lifetime

46

Number of eggs laid by some fish

Ling	28,360,000
Turbot	9,000,000
Cod	6,650,000
Halibut	2,750,000
Common carp	2,500,000
Flounder	1,330,000
Sole	570,000
Plaice	500,000
Haddock	250,000
Herring	50,000
Mackerel	50,000

For each pound of its body weight a twenty pound (0.45 kg) salmon will lay 600–700 eggs.

Two Stupid Fishermen

Two stupid fishermen were fishing from a river bank when a dead duck floated by. "How sad," one fisherman said. "A dead duck." … "Where?" said the other dumb fisherman looking up to the sky.

* * *

A Stupid Fisherman

A stupid fisherman won a gold medal in a fishing competition … and had it bronzed.

* * *

A Dumb Fisherman

A dumb fisherman wanted to go fishing so he made for the nearest frozen lake and started to make a circular cut in the ice. Suddenly from the sky a voice said: "There are no fish under the ice!"

Startled, the dumb fisherman moves on down the frozen lake and starts to cut another hole. Again, the voice from above rings out: "There are no fish under the ice!"

A third time he moves on and a third time he cuts a hole. This time a voice booms out: "There are no fish under the ice!"

The dumb fisherman is now quite worried and looks skyward and says: "Lord, Lord is that you?"

"No!" the voice booms back. "This is the ice-rink manager!"

DID YOU KNOW?

The eggs of a whale shark are as big as rugby balls.

*

The empty egg case of the thornback ray is known as a mermaid's purse.

*

Before a salmon becomes an adult it is first called an ova, then an alevin, then a parr, then a smolt.

*

The fish with the longest name is
Humuhumu nukunuku apuaa from Hawaii
and is commonly known as the triggerfish.

*

A kingfisher makes its nest with fish bones.
And a baby kingfisher can eat about 150 small fish during the three to four weeks it is in the nest.
That's about 37.5 fish a week for a single chic!

*

The archerfish can send a jet of water up to five metres through the air.

*

The turkeyfish is the most ornamental in the world.

*

The parrotfish spins a "nightgown" around itself before it settles down for the night.

The Fish That Killed A King

LAMPREY

Petromyzon Harinus

Like its cousin the hagfish, lampreys are parasitic. This eel-like fish has no jaws and has horny teeth set in a circular mouth. They attach themselves to their prey and rasp away at the flesh while sucking in their blood. They have an anticoagulant in their saliva that keeps the victim's blood fluid.

It has become established in the Great Lakes of Canada and the U.S.A. and is a serious threat to the fishing industry.

Status – Not Threatened

* * *

Henry the first of England (1068–1135) died at St Denis in Normandy on the first of December 1135 after eating too much of his favourite food – lamprey. Henry was 66 and had ruled England for 35 years.

HAGFISH

Myxine Glutinosa

Ranked among the most repulsive fish, this eel-like fish has no scales, no bones and is jawless. Its skeleton is made entirely of cartilage and with its eyes just under its skin, it is almost blind. It can produce a slime so sticky and gooey that it can suffocate a predator by clogging up its gills.

Their circular jawless mouth has eight barbells and their tongues have rows of razor sharp horny teeth. They feed by attaching themselves to their prey and rasping away at their flesh. They will burrow right into the body of their victim secreting the sticky slime to protect themselves against the digestive juices of their hosts. They devour everything, sometimes leaving the host skin intact with nothing inside but bare bones.

This gruesome fish is found world wide and live at depths of four hundred feet.

Status – Not Threatened

* * *

SALMON

Salmo Salar

The life history of the salmon is similar to that of the sea trout. But while the sea trout feed in fresh water, the salmon rarely, if ever does. Nevertheless, it can still be "teased" to take artificial flies, spinners, plugs, and natural baits (prawns and sprats) mounted on special flights. A large growing fish of immense strength, sometimes caught to weights topping 40lbs.

Status – Not Threatened

The salmon returning to the river of their birth may have a journey of up to 1,500 miles to the shallow gravel pits where they were born. Travelling perhaps only five miles a day facing waterfalls, dams, and all kinds of predators, including man. But they will never turn back as their sole aim is to reach the place of their birth; there to lay and fertilize their eggs and to die.

The Native People of the North West Coast of America

The native people of the north west coast of America endow the salmon with spiritual qualities and refer to themselves as the "salmon people." When the salmon is seen returning to the gravel pits they were born in, joyous celebrations are held in honour of the great salmon spirit and a ritual laying of a complete set of salmon bones from the previous year's catch are laid reverently into the river and the following prayer is recited:

'Welcome swimmer! I thank you because I am still alive this season when you came back to our good place; for the reason why you came back is that we might play together with my fishing tackle. Now you go home and tell your friends that you had good luck on the account of your coming home: And that they shall come with their wealth: and that I may get some of their wealth.'

*

The Bella Coola People

The Bella Coola people of the Pacific north west in British Columbia, Canada believed that salmon were not fish but people who lived in a magic village beneath the sea. They also held a belief that twins were due to a salmon entering the body, and that twins had the power to persuade the return of the salmon by throwing gifts of wooden salmon carved from red cedar wood, into the river.

Fintan the Salmon

On the banks of the river Boyne lived Finegas an old and wise Druid who had, for years, tried to catch Fintan the salmon of knowledge who dwelt in a dark pool of the river under a hazel tree whose nuts of knowledge dropped into the river when Fintan would eat them. It was said that whoever ate off Fintan would possess the wisdom of all ages.

One day Finegas caught Fintan and gave him to Finn McCool to cook, bidding Finn not to eat of Fintan himself. When the fish was cooked Finn McCool bought it to Finegas. The old Druid looked at Finn and saw in his eyes the knowledge he had spent many years searching for. He asked Finn, "Have you eaten of Fintan?"

"No," said Finn McCool, "But when I turned him on the spit his juices burnt my thumb which I sucked to ease the pain."

"Take the Salmon of knowledge and eat of him, for in thee the prophecy has come true," said the old and wise Druid.

From that day on when Finn McCool wished to know what would befall, he would put his thumb in his mouth and all the knowledge of Fintan the salmon was his.

* * *

Salmon in 1679

In 1679 salmon was so plentiful in England that it was food only for apprentices and servant who stipulated that they should not be obliged to feed on it more than five time a week.

*

* But *

I, When I

Undress Me

Each Night Upon My

Knees, Will Pray

The Lord To

To Bless

Me

With

Salmon Pie And Cheese

A salmon in spawning is called a kipper
Kipper: Smoked and salted herring
Kipper Period: A slack time in trade
Done up like a kipper: Totally and utterly deceived
All Kippers and curtains: a snob.

Kippers: short for – kids in parent's pockets eroding
retirement savings.

If Smoking is bad for you, how come it cures kippers?

* * *

THE CANOEIST

A canoeist who was paddling down a calm stretch of river
was enjoying the scenery when a loud splash broke the
silence around him. A magnificent salmon had leaped from
the water ahead. Twelve strokes later the canoe crossed the
ever widening circle made by the salmon. Twelve strokes
after that it passed through the circle on the other side. As he
paddled on he tried to calculate how far away (in strokes) the
salmon had been at the moment it jumped.

How far was it?

Answer on page 151

56

ORANGE ROUGHY

Hoplostethus Atlanticus

The orange roughy was first discovered in vast uncountable numbers by Australian and New Zealand fishermen in the 1970s. Living at depths of over 800 metres, they were little known at the time, but in less than no time fishermen were taking about 40,000 tonnes of roughy a year. Then marine scientists discovered a disturbing fact – the orange roughy are extremely long lived. Some may live to over 150 years and may only breed once in their lifetime.

Roughys eaten today may have been born in the reign of Queen Victoria. By the time this fact was discovered the population of the roughy was in serious trouble. Today there are strict quotas on the amount of roughy that can be taken. In 2000/2001 the allowable commercial catch (T.A.C.C.) was set at just over 15,000 metric tonnes a year. But even with good management it will be decades before the orange roughy recovers; if they ever do.

Status – Threatened

* * *

PIRARUCA

Arapaima Giggas

A leftover from pre-history, this massive fish is considered to be one of the world's largest fish. It is called the "Redfish" by the native Indians of the Amazon because the reddish coloured scales and can grow to lengths of fourteen to fifteen feet.

Although a fish of fourteen to fifteen feet (plus), it would be rare because of its great food value.

They belong to the family osteo-glossidae; meaning "boney tongue". The Piraruca's tongue is six to seven inches long and covered in tiny rasp-like teeth which the Indians use for grating manioc and coconuts. The pink flesh is cut into strips, dried and salted and is known as the bacon of the Amazon.

The Piraruca lays up to 47,000 eggs which are incubated in the mouth by the male.

Status – Endangered/Extinct in many parts of its range

* * *

Song Of The Shetland Fishers

Sir Walter Scott
1771-1832

Farewell, merry maidens, to song,
 And to laugh,
For the brave lads of westra are
 Bound for the haaf;
And we must have labour, and hunger,
 And pain,
Ere we dance with the maids of
 Dunrossness again.

For now, in our trim boats of Noroway
 Deal,
We must dance on the waves, with
 The porpoise and seal;
The breeze it shall pipe, so it pipe not
 Too high,
And the gull be our songstress when-
 e'er she flits by.

Sing on, my brave bird, while we
 Follow, like thee,
By bank, shoal, and quicksand, the
 Swarms of the sea;
And when twenty-score fishes are
 Straining our line,
Sing louder, brave bird, for their spoils
 Shall be thine.

We'll sing while we bait, and we'll
 Sing while we haul
For the deep of the haaf have enough
 For us all;
There is torsk for the gentle, and
 Skate for the carle,
And there's a wealth for magnus,
 The son of the earl.

Huzza! My brave comrades, give way
      For the haaf,
We shall sooner come back to the
      Dance and the laugh;
For life without mirth is a lamp
      Without oil;
Then, mirth and lone life to the bold
      Magnus troil!

COD-NUNDRUMS

*

* TO *

ARE TO

RESOLUTIONS

CATCH TO HARD

ON EELS

HANG

LIKE

EASY BUT

```
                    *

                 *  A  *

              IS OYSTER

              LIKE FISH

                 NUT

                 AN

              A BUILT




                    *

              *  THE  *

           FROM SPENT NOT

           DEDUCT GODS

           DO HOURS

              MAN'S

              SPAN

              THE

           FISHING ALLOTTED
```

Answers on page 150

THE OLD MAN

It was a cold winter's day. An old man walked out onto a frozen lake, cut a hole in the ice, dropped in his fishing line and waited patiently for a bite. He was there for almost an hour without even a nibble when a young boy walked out onto the ice, and cut a hole in the ice next to him. The young boy dropped in his fishing line and within minutes hooked a large bass. The old man couldn't believe his eyes but put it down to plain luck.

Shortly after, the boy pulled put another large bass. He kept catching fish after fish. Finally, the old man could take it no longer.

"Son," he said, "I've been here over an hour without a nibble. You've been here only a few minutes and caught half a dozen fish! How do you do it!"

The boy responded: "Roo faf, roo reep ra rums rarrm."

"Look!" said the old man. "I can't understand a word you're saying."

The boy spat into his hand and said: "You have to keep the worms warm!"

THE YOUNG ANGLERS

A couple of young anglers were fishing at their special pond off the beaten track when suddenly a gamekeeper jumps out of the bushes. Immediately one of the young anglers throws down his rod and starts running through the woods with the gamekeeper hot on his heels. After about half a mile the young angler stops to catch his breath.

"Let me see your licence, boy!" wheezed the gamekeeper. With that, the young angler takes out his wallet and gives the gamekeeper a valid fishing license.

"You must be as silly as a box of tricks," says the gamekeeper. "You don't have to run from me if you have a valid licence!"

"Yes sir I know," said the young angler. "But my friend back there, well, he don't have one…"

62

A Fine Line

*

* THERE *
IS A FINE LINE
BETWEEN FISHING
AND STANDING ON
THE RIVER
BANK
AND
LOOKING
LIKE
AN IDIOT

To Be An Angler

*

* All *

you need

to be an angler

is the capacity

for calm, self-

possessed

wait-

ing

and …

A maggot.

COD

Gadus Morhua

Small cod, known as codling and weighing under 6lbs, supply east coast beach anglers with top class fishing throughout the winter. Bigger cod, fish of 15–50lb, are more often caught from boat marks along the eastern corner of England and far down the southern coastline.

The biggest Atlantic cod ever caught weighed 211lb … an absolute giant. The average weight of an Atlantic cod is between 15 and 50lb. It was estimated that this monster cod would provide over two hundred meals.

There once was a time, off the north coast of America, that fishermen needed neither net nor line to catch cod. Such was their number that all that was needed was baskets with which to scoop them up. So dense were they, it was said that a man could walk on them and not get his feet wet. They were thought to be inexhaustible.

By 1960, however, the number of spawning cod had dropped to 1.6 million tonnes and by 1990 they had sunk even further to just 22,000 tonnes. Then, in 1992, fishing for cod off the coast of north America was stopped altogether. Commercially, cod was extinct. According to reports in 2002, stocks of cod had still not made a comeback.

Status – Vulnerable

CODSWALLOP!

Codswallop has nothing to do with
the cod fish (gadus morhau).

In 1872 a Mr Hiram C Codd set up a business selling lemonade in small glass bottles with marble stoppers. At this time it was safer to drink beer than it was water. Some beers were very low in alcohol content, the weakest beer was known as wallop. Hiram C's lemonade was so weak it became known as Codd's Wallop. Today, we still refer to a pint of weak beer as a pint of cod's or a pint of wallop. It is also a term to describe something of little or no value. Worthless. Rubbish.

A load of old codswallop!

THE FAIRY
Unknown

A fairy went to market
And bought a little fish
She put it in a crystal bowl
Upon a golden dish

An hour she sat in wonderment
And watched its silver gleam
And then she gently took it up
And slipped it in a stream

I WISH I WERE A LITTLE FISH
Unknown

I wish I were a little fish,
To swim, now fast, now slow,
All round about the wide blue sea,
As far as I could go.

I want to see the whelks that crawl
Along in sandy rows,
And watch the lobsters and the crabs
All eating with their toes.

I want to see the fishes nurse
Their little boys and girls,
And peep inside the oyster shells
To see them making pearls.

CARDINAL SCORPIONFISH

Scorpaena Cardinalis

With thirteen poisonous spines on backs and around their head, these fish need careful handling. A scratch from the spines can cause pain to travel up the arm and over the chest in less than an hour causing violent vomiting and collapse.

The flesh of the cardinal fish is good eating, but great care is still taken when filleting the dead fish. Cautious fishermen will not allow it on their boats.

Status – Not Threatened

* * *

STONEFISH

Synanceia Verrucosa
Synanceia Trachynis

Known as the horrendous one and the warty one, these two almost identical fish are the ugliest of all fish. They are covered in slime and algae and have up to fourteen spines on their backs. The tips of these spines are so sharp that the slightest touch will cause them to puncture the skin. The poison from these spines can kill a person in about four hours. But before death, the pain can be so agonising it can cause insanity. Even survival is unpleasant; excruciating pain can last for days. If they've been touched or trodden on, fingers and toes can turn black and drop off. Unpleasant side effects can last for a year or more afterwards.

Status – Venerable / Endangered

ANGRY BEES

Swansea coastguards were called out to rescue an angler after his boat had been invaded by a swarm of angry bees. The coastguard's secret weapon to deal with this problem? A beekeeper!

HIPPOS

Two anglers dozing in the sun on a riverbank in Ormsk, Russia woke to find they were surrounded by two hippos that had escaped from a nearby zoo.

FISHING HOOKS

Food fishing goes back to prehistoric times when primitive man would fish with almost anything: by hand, club, spear, and nets made from grass and reeds. Later the primitive man made hooks from stone, shell and cactus spines. Over the centuries the hook has changed little and the early fisherman would instantly recognise today's steel wire hooks.

FISHING LINES

Until the 17th century, fishing lines were tied to the end of a pole. Then it was learnt how to use a running line with a reel. Fishing lines could now be cast further out and could sink deeper.

BAD EYES

A man rings his boss and says, "I can't come into work today."

"Why not?" asks the boss.

"It's my eyes," said the man.

"What's wrong with your eyes?" asks the boss.

"I just can't see myself coming into work today, so I'm going fishing instead."

* * *

WHY DO FISH HAVE SCALES, DAD?

A father takes his son on a fishing trip. After a couple of hours out in the boat, the boy becomes curious about the world around him. He asks his father:

"How does this boat float, Dad?"

"I don't rightly know, son," said the father.

A little later the boy asks: "Why do fish have scales, Dad?"

"I don't rightly know, son," said the father.

"How do fish breathe under water, Dad?"

"I don't rightly know, son," said the father.

After a few minutes had passed the boy says: "You don't mind me asking all these questions do you, Dad?"

"Of course not, son," said the father. "If you don't ask questions you'll never learn anything."

THOMAS BIRCH

The eighteenth-century scholar Thomas Birch was a keen angler. But, never very successful and rarely caught anything, so he made himself an outfit that made him look like a tree in the hope that he could lull the fish into thinking he was not there. His disguise didn't work, he still caught nothing!

But he took in good heart the jokes played on him by friends who would picnic beneath his leafy branches.

But dogs – well, they were a different kettle of fish!

EDMOND HALEY

In 1686 Edmond Haley (he of the comet fame) accepted a position as a clerk with the Royal Society with a salary of £50 per annum.

At around this time the Society had backed the publication of an enormous and costly flop called *The History of Fishes*, leaving the Society with a big financial headache. Haley was informed that they could not pay him the promised £50 per annum but, instead, they would pay him in copies of *The History of Fishes*.

AMBULANCE ANGLING CHAMPIONSHIP

In 1972 two hundred ambulance personnel from all over Gt. Britain gathered at a canal in Kidderminster Worcestershire for the national ambulance personnel's angling championships. The competition was to last five hours but after three hours of keenly competitive fishing not one fish had been caught.

A local resident passing by saw the frustration of the anglers and informed them that the fish had been moved upstream three weeks earlier so that the stretch of canal they were fishing in could be repaired!

COD - NUNDRUMS

*

* IS *

YOU WHEN

DO FISHING

CAN'T

LIFE

YOU

GO

SOMETHING

*

* IF *

HOME

SHOWED MUCH

WHEN EASIER AT

AS FISHING AS

PATIENCE BE

LIVING DO

WOULD

MUCH

THEY

THEY'RE MEN

Answers page 150

CELEBRITY FISH

COD STEWART
PRAWN CONNERY
SKATE MOSS
SEAN BREAM
KYLIE MINNOW
FINNY DRIVER
M C HAMMERHEAD
ERROL FIN
DICK VAN PIKE
ELVERS PRESLEY
MARLIN BRANDO
MUSSEL CROW
SIR CLIFF PILCHARD
DIANA WRASS
LING CROSBY
NAT KING SOLE
MARVIN RAY
SPRATS DOMINO
STATUS KOI
GREGORY PIKE
GOLDIE PRAWN

AESOP'S FABLES

A cook laid some fish in a pan and started to fry them. As soon as the fish began to feel the heat one of them cried: "There's no enduring this!" So they all jumped into the fire and were worse off than before.

* * *

A fisherman went to fish a river and, having laid his nets across the steam, he tied a stone to a long cord and beat the water on either side of the net; so as to drive the fish into the meshes. Someone who lived thereabouts saw him at work and complained that he was stirring up the mud and making the water unfit to drink.

"I'm sorry," said the fisherman. "But if I don't disturb the water I shall starve to death – and it will be your fault."

* * *

A hunter returning from the mountains after a successful day, met a fisherman with a creel of fish. The hunter had a partiality for fish, while the fisherman preferred game; so they exchanged the contents of their baskets. This they continued to do for a long while, and dined with all the more pleasure, until someone remarked: "If these fellows go on like this their palates will grow stale, and each will want to return to his own catch."

* * *

An angler, who depended for his living upon rod and line, had caught one little fish at the end of a long day's fruitless toil. "Please have mercy on me," said the fish, "I'm too small to make you a square meal. I'm not yet full grown; so throw me back into the water, and then, when I'm larger and worth eating, you can come back and catch me again."

"Not likely," the man replied; "I've got you now, and if I let you go your tune will be 'Catch me if you can'."

CODFISH NAMED MUIR

A prudish old cod named Muir
Had a mind so incredibly pure
At a Pike's house one day
She fainted away
At the sight of a sea-horses manure

*

A SHARK NAMED TED

There was a young shark named Ted
Who always ate seaweed in bed
Till his mother said: 'Teddy
Don't you think you are ready
To start eating people instead?'

*

TERRIFIED HAKES

The one thing that terrifies hakes
Is that they land up as cheap fish-cakes;
They only dream
Of being simmered in cream
Or baked to a turn as hake-steaks

HAKE

Steindachneria Argentea

This one foot (30 cm) fish has large eyes, large mouth, and sharp teeth. The hake is an extremely cannibalistic fish. Fifty per cent of its diet is made up of its own species. They are night hunters using their large eyes to locate their prey in the darkness striking with a savage snap-and-bite form of attack.

Status – Not Threatened

* * *

BABY HAKE

As I was walking near a lake
I met a little baby hake
He ate so much of jelly cake
He made his little belly ache

* * *

TOBIAS

Here lies Tobias our dear cat
Who breathed his last upon the mat
His death was due to cook's mistake
In giving him our processed hake
The moral's plain
It is no treat
For pets to have what humans eat

THE GAMEKEEPER

A gamekeeper on a country estate stopped a man with two buckets of fish as he was leaving a lake that was well known for its fishing.

"Do you have a licence to catch those fish, sir?" asked the gamekeeper.

"No, sir," said the man. "These are my pet fish."

"Pet fish?" asked the gamekeeper.

"Yes, sir," said the man. "Every night I bring them down to the lake and let them have a swim around, and when I think they have had long enough I give them a whistle and they jump back into the bucket and I take them home."

"Are you trying to take me for a fool, sir?" asks the gamekeeper.

"I'll show you," said the man pouring the fish into the lake.

After a few minutes the gamekeeper says: "Well?"

"Well what?" said the man.

"When are you going to call them back?" said the gamekeeper.

"Call who back?" said the man.

"The fish," said the gamekeeper.

"What fish?" said the man.

* * *

A WAIF'S PRAYER
JACE
Brian Stephen Waters
1942 –

*

*   Bless   *
this tiny little
fish lying forlornly
on my dish bless
this hard
unbuttered
toast
Father
Son
And
Holy Ghost

*

* A *
Handsome
young flounder
Named Jace fell
In love with a beautiful
Plaice he loved her
Quite dearly
And kissed
Her twice
Yearly
That
Handsome
Young flounder named Jace

CATS

Cats are often blamed when fish go missing from ponds, but cats have an intense dislike of water and only strike out if it feels it has a good chance of catching something. An old sickly fish may well fall victim. But a healthy fish will be much too fast for the striking paw of a cat.

The cat would eat fish but would not get her feet wet.

Proverb

* * *

FROGS

Frogs are extremely unlikely to cause harm to fish. But during frogs' breeding season this lovelorn amphibian will grab onto anything that moves causing injury or even death to a fish.

* * *

BIRDS

Birds are the biggest threat to a fish pond. A passing gull may try for a fish or two and if you live close to a river or stream, his majesty the kingfisher may pay your pond a royal visit. But the robber baron of fish ponds is the heron. Feeding at daybreak you may never see a heron at your pool side, but if you are losing fish regularly, it may well be the heron.

FINSULTS

COD'S EYES
COD'S HEAD
FISH LIPS
FISH FACE
FISH FART
FISH BREATH
KIPPER FEET
STUPID KIPPER
OLD TROUT
TROUT FACE
TROUT POUT

*

You've got a face like a happy haddock (miserable).

The last time I saw a mouth like that it had a hook in it.

Is that a cod's head on your shoulder or am I seeing double?

The fry of the Australian snapper fish
(chrysephrys auratus) is called a Cockney.

Salmon and trout	**Stout** (beers)
Flounder and dab	**Cab** (taxi)
Jack the rippers	**Kippers**
Pair of kippers	**Slippers**
Herring and kipper	**Stripper**
Lillian Gish	**Fish**
Fisherman's daughter	**Water**
Fillet of cod	**God**

THE BLEED'N TRAHT
Nonsense Rhyme
Brian Stephen Waters
1942-

There was a bleed'n traht wot
Lived up a bleed'n spaht,
One day the bleed'n rain pours dahn
An' washes the bleeder aht.

An' as 'e layed 'arf drahnd
Dahn in the bleed'n street
'e cursed the bleed'n rain for
such a bleed'n treat

Just then the bleed'n sun comes aht
An' up dries the bleed'n rain
An' so the bleed'n little traht
Shoots up the spaht again.

Then up comes a bleed'n fisherman
Who espies 'im in 'is snuggery
An' sharpens up 'is bleed'n 'ooks
An' rips 'im aht by thuggery!

An' then a bleed'n snooty type
Wha' 'ad a bleed'n gun
'e sees the bleed'n fisherman
An' shoots 'is bleed'n fun.

*

The moral of me story
Is plain to all an' one –
That w'en yer up the bleed'n spaht
Yer get no bleed'n fun.

EDWARD LEAR
1812-1888

*

* THERE *

WAS

A YOUNG LADY

FROM WALES WHO

CAUGHT LARGE FISH

WITHOUT ANY SCALES

WHEN SHE LIFTED

HER HOOK SHE

EXCLAIMED

"ONLY

LOOK"

THE

ESTACTIC

YOUNG

LADY FROM WALES

The Four Swordsmen Of The Ocean

SWORDFISH
Xiphias Gladius

The swordfish can reach speeds of up to 60 mph (96.56 kph) and have been known to plunge their "sword" or "spike" through nearly twenty-two inches of wood. It has been reported that small boats have been sunk when the swordfish have pierced their hulls, although it is not believed that swordfish deliberately attack boats; but that it is their inability to stop when swimming at high speeds. The swordfish can grow twelve to thirteen feet (396.24cm) in length.

Status – Endangered

* * *

SAILFISH
Istiophorus Plstypterus

The sailfish gets its name from the large dorsal fin that runs along its back. The "sail" is only used to balance the fish when resting. When it's ready to move it folds the "sail" into a groove along its back and sets off at a tremendous speed, reaching a top speed of 60 mph (109.43 kph). Its "sword" or "spike" is quite small and it uses it to stab its prey. A full grown sailfish can reach a length of ten feet (304.8cm).

Status – Threatened / Endangered

MARLIN

Tetrapterus Albidus

The marlin also has a "sail" and uses it in much the same way as its cousin the sailfish. Its small "sword" or "spike" reminded sailors of the marlin spike they used to secure the rigging of their ships. The blue marlin of the Atlantic can grow to nearly thirteen feet (396.24cm). The black marlin of the Pacific can reach lengths of fifteen feet (457.2cm)

* * *

Status – Threatened

SAWFISH

Pristis Microdon

The sawfish is the odd man out among the swordsmen. Unlike the swordfish, sailfish and the marlin who are all related, the sawfish is a member of the ray family. Rather than "sword" it has a "saw" with up to thirty-eight teeth along each side of the cutting edge. It uses its "saw" to lash out and impale its prey. It then takes its impaled victims to the sea-bed where it dines at its leisure. The "saw" is also used to dig out shellfish. The sawfish can grow to twenty eight feet (853.44cm) long.

Status – Endangered

The Song of the Fisherman's Wife

Alfred, Lord Tennyson
1809-1892

Sweet and low, sweet and low.
Wind of the western sea,
Low, low, breath and blow,
Wind of the western sea!
Over the rolling waters go,
Come from the dying moon, and blow
Blow him again to me.

Sleep and rest, sleep and rest,
Father will come to thee soon;
Rest, rest, on mother's breast,
Father will come to thee soon;
Father will come to his babe in the nest,
Silver sails all out of the west,
Under the silver moon;
Sleep, my little one, sleep my pretty one, sleep.

COD - NUNDRUMS

*
* Die *
Way Never
Old That Smell
They
Just
Fisherman

*
* You *
Catch
Fish Really
Don't Any-
Thing
Never
For
Compliments

Answers page 150

THE OLD LADY WHO LIVED IN A SHOE

It was Friday night and the old lady who lived in a shoe decided to give her children a treat by buying them fish and chips for their supper. The total bill at the chippy came to twenty-five pounds. When she got home she unwrapped five pounds worth of chips and half as many pieces again of cod and haddock.

If the fish cost a pound a piece, how many pieces of cod and how many pieces of haddock did she buy?

Answers on page 151

CATFISH STINK BAIT

A woman goes into a shop to buy a rod and reel as a gift. She doesn't know which one to get so she just grabs one and goes over to the counter where there's a shop assistant wearing dark glasses.

"Excuse me, sir," she says. "Can you tell me anything about this rod and reel?"

The assistant replies, "Madam, I'm blind but if you drop the rod and reel on the counter I can tell you everything you need to know from the sound they make."

She doesn't believe him but drops them on the counter anyway. He says, "That's a 6-foot graphite rod with a Zebco reel and a 10lb test line … It's a good all round rod and reel and it's only £20!"

The lady said. "It's amazing that you can tell all that just by the sound of them dropping on the counter. I think it's just what I'm looking for. I'll take them."

The assistant turns to the till to ring up the sale; as he does, so she breaks wind big time. At first she is embarrassed, but realises there is no way he could tell it was her … being he wouldn't know she was the only person in the shop.

The assistant rings up the sale and says, "That will be £25.50."

The woman says, "But you said it was only £20."

"Yes, madam, the rod and reel is £20, but the duck call is £3.00 and the catfish stink bait is £2.50."

* * *

The Fishing Fleet
Frances A Greenwood

Into the misty pearly dawn
The fishermen sail away.
Far out from the shore they cast their nets
Where the deep fishes play.

When evening shadows softly fall
On the surging billow's foam
Gladly they turn their heavy boats
And sail again for home.

Edward Lear
1812-1888

*
* There *
Was
an old person
of Dundalk who
tried to teach fishes
to walk when they
tumbled down
dead he got
weary and
said
"I had
better
go back
to Dundalk."

THE FISH-MAN

Around their camp fires, Native Americans told stories of how their ancestors lived in a cold and barren land where they were always cold and hungry.

One day a fish-man appeared close to the shore singing a sweet and beautiful song. From the waist up he looked just like a man, but from the waist down instead of legs he had two tails joined together. He sang of a land he knew where food was plentiful and the climate warm, and that if they put their trust in him he would take them there.

The Indians were suspicious of the fish-man and took council on what to do. They realised that if they stayed they would die of cold and hunger. So the council agreed that they had to put their trust in the fish-man.

Gathering up the last of their food, they set sail in the wake of the fish-man. After weeks of sailing the fish-man stopped swimming and pointed ahead. On the horizon was the dark outline of land. They had arrived on what we now know to be the north coast of the United States of America.

The fish-man had been true to his word, game was plentiful, and delicious fruits hung from every tree and bush, and the rivers abounded with multitudes of fish. They were happy and made the land their own, but what the fish-man had not told them was that their beautiful land would one day be taken from them by a white race of people from the other side of the world.

DO?

Do zebra fish see everything in black and white?

Will a clown fish make you laugh?

Do angelfish have halos?

Are skate good on skateboards?

Do carp keep on, and on, and on?

Why are snapper fish snappy?

Are groupers groupies?

Can a tuna sing in tune?

Do dogfish fight with catfish?

Do starfish only come out at night?

Do jellyfish like custard?

Can flying fish do loop de loops?

Can a conga eel dance the conga?

Are goldfish wealthy?

Can a seahorse canter?

Do swordfish fence?

Is a lionfish full of pride?

Do soles have soul mates?

Do blowfish blow their own trumpets?

Does a bloater always feel bloated?

Do all the fish in the sea pray to almighty cod?

MOSS LEA

Moss lea near Oldham, Lancashire claim to have opened the first fish and chip shop in 1863 but a counter claim from London say that one was opened there in 1860.

*

CHIPS

George Crum first cooked potatoes as chips in the 1860s. And chips soon replaced bread as the main accompaniment with fried fish.

*

WWII

During World War Two the only food not rationed in the UK was fish and chips.

*

OLDEST TAKE AWAY

In Britain we eat an estimated three million fish and chip dinners a year in an estimated eight thousand fish and chip shops across the United Kingdom. It is Britain's oldest and best loved take away.

A PORTION OF COD & CHIPS

A portion of cod and chips has less than half the fat of
chicken tikka masala and pilau rice
or
sweet and sour pork with egg fried rice.

* * *

OMEGA 3

Fish contains the essential fatty acid omega-3 along with
other vitamins, minerals and amino acids in protein. Oily fish
has what you need for the development of the nerves, eyes
and brain. Children who don't consume enough fatty acid can
have poor memory, dyslexia, behavioural problems, learning
difficulties and sometimes, hyperactivity. One serving of oily
fish a week is recommended. Shellfish is a good source of
zinc; a crucial mineral for memory and concentration. Even
a mild deficiency can affect the way a child's brain works;
leading to irritability, mood swings and loss of appetite.

YOU "COD" NOT MAKE IT UP

Fish and chip shops around the U. K.

HUNKY DORY
Gravesend, Kent

* *

FISHCOTHEQUE
Waterloo, London

* *

FRIED OF PLAICE
Sevenoaks, Kent

* *

THE FISHICIAN
Newton Le Willows, Lancs

* *

THE COD-FATHER
Stevenage, Herts

* *

IN COD WE TRUST
Grimthorpe, York

* *

THE ALMIGHTY COD
Southmead, Bristol

* *

A FISH CALLED RHONDA
South Wales

THY GIFT OF FISH & CHIPS

Allan Michael Laing

We thank thee, Lord, for vulgar food
For trotters, tripe, pig's cheek,
For steak and onions with their crude
But appetizing reek.

Potatoes in their jacket make
Us plain folk honour thee;
And thou art with us when we bake
Fresh shrimps for Sunday tea.

Thy people's praise is overdue,
But see, dear Lord, we kneel
To offer thanks for Irish stew
And tasty cheap cowheel.

Now wait a minute, Lord! Don't miss
The last words on our lips;
We thank thee most of all for this,
Thy gift of fish and chips.

* * *

FISH FINGERS

Birds Eye Fish Fingers were fifty years old on the 26th of
September 2005. Over 87 million Fish Fingers are sold each
year in the United Kingdom.

DON'T ASK FOR BREAD
Anon

A wretched man walked up and down
To buy his dinner in the town.

At last he found a wretched place
And entered with a modest grace,

Took off his coat, took off his hat,
And wiped his feet upon the mat,

Took out his purse to count his pence
And found he had but two half-cents.

The bill of fare, he scanned it through
To see what two half-cents would do

The only item of them all
For two half-cents was one fishball.

So to the waiter he did call
And gently whispered: 'One fishball.'

The waiter bellowed down the hall,
'This gentleman here wants one fishball.'

The diners looked both one and all
To see who wanted one fishball.

The wretched man, all ill at ease,
Said, 'A little bread, sir, if you please.'

The waiter bellowed down the hall:
'We don't serve bread with one fishball!'

The wretched man, he felt so small,
He quickly left the dining hall.

The wretched man, he went outside
And shot himself, until he died.

This is the moral of it all,
Don't ask for bread with one fishball.

*

HERRING

Clupea Harengus (Atlantic)
Clupea Pallasii (Pacific)

Herring are known to have as many as three thousand million
fish in one shoal. A female herring can lay up to 50,000 eggs
at one spawning. So, if we assume that half the three thousand
million shoals of herring are female (one thousand, five
hundred million) they will lay a staggering seven hundred
and fifty trillion eggs. But only one per cent of this vast
amount of eggs will survive into adulthood.

Status – Threatened, due to over-fishing

*

A RED HERRING

To mislead or distract

A herring when dried, salted and smoked will turn a reddish
brown colour (a kipper) and will have a particularly strong
smell. In medieval times they were useful as lures for training
young hounds in stag hunting.

In the 1800s fox lovers tried to confuse hunting hounds by
dragging a red herring across the trail of a fox in an attempt
to divert the hounds away from their quarry.

The Herring Caller

The most boring job in fishing history must be that of the herring caller, who in Victorian times would sit and look out to sea for endless hours scanning the horizon for flocks of gulls that would indicate schools of herring. When the herring caller sighted the gulls he would simply call out in a loud voice; "Herring! Herring!" The fishermen would then set sail to catch the herring fish. When the fishing fleet returned with their catch of herring, the herring caller would go back to sitting for endless hours looking out to sea for flocks of gulls.

* * *

Scientists have found that
Herring can communicate
With each other at night
By
Breaking
Wind.

HERRINGS' HEAD
Circa 1831

Now what shall we do with the herrings' head?
Turn them into loaves of bread

Herrings' head—loaves of bread and all such things.

Of all the fish in the sea
The herring's the king of fish for me.

And what shall we do with the herrings' eyes?
Turn them into puddings and pies.

And what shall we do with the herrings' backs?
Turn them into fishing smacks.

And what shall we do with herrings' fins?
Turn them into needles and pins.

And what shall we do with the herrings' bellies?
Turn them into jam and jellies.

And what shall we do with the herrings' tails-?
Turn them into buckets and pails.

And what shall we do with the herrings' guts?
Turn them into comic cuts.

Herrings' guts—comic cuts,
Herrings' tails—buckets and pails,
Herrings' bellies—jam and jelly,
Herrings' fins—needles and pins,
Herrings' backs—fishing smacks,
Herrings' eyes—puddings and pies,
Herrings' heads—loaves of bread and all such things.

Of all the fish that's in the sea
The herring's the king of fish for me.

Major Colour Types Of Koi Carp

Tancho-Kohaku   –   White body, red markings on head

Shiro-Muji   –   White body

Hariwake   –   Silver body, gold markings

Shiro-Bekko   –   White body, black markings

Kohaich   –   White body, red markings

Sanke   –   Black body, white and red markings

Hajiro   –   Black body

Asagi   –   Blue scaly back, orange belly and markings

Ohgon   –   Golden body

Koi carp come in all sizes and can cost anything from a small fortune to a large fortune.

Status   –   Not Threatened

* * *

FISHY MOVIES

Marlin Rouge

Jurassic Carp

Pulp Fishing

The Codfather

Home Abalone

Forrest Guppy

Kiss Me Skate

Analyse Sprat

Krill Bill

Cods of War

Licence to Krill

Tiddler on the Roof

Eel Met by Moonlight

The Ray of the Jackal

Four Whitings And A Funeral

Honey I Shrunk The Squids

Silence Of The Lampreys

SHADE OF A TREE

*

* I *

Like to

Fish in the

Shade of a

Tree

And

Soak

Up the sun

ENDORSE

*

* Ho *

you who've

been a-fishing

Will endorse me

when I say that it

always is

the biggest

fish you

catch

that

gets away

THE TOWN COUNCIL OF ACWORTH

The town council of Acworth, twenty-four miles outside Atlanta, Georgia U.S.A. passed a city ordinance requiring all households to own a fishing rod.

*

It is possible to fish in four American states
from one point on the San Juan river:

UTAH
COLORADO
ARIZONA
NEW MEXICO

*

* The *
urchin with
pin and string
Can chum with million-
aire and King;
Vain pride
is a
for-
gotten
thing
Out angling

J.M. Webb

ST NEOT

Patron Saint Of Fish

Born? Died 877
Feast Day – July 21
St Neot is known as the Pygmy Saint

The height of St Neot varies from fifteen inches to four feet tall. Either way he was a small man. He was renowned for his love of animals and birds.

One day an angel appeared before Neot and gave him three fishes telling him that if he only ate one at a time there would always be three. One day, Neot became ill and took to his bed. His servant, not knowing what the angel had commanded, took two fish from the well and cooked them just the way Neot like them. When the servant laid the fish before Neot, the saint was horrified and began to pray over the dead fish. After an hour of prayer he returned them to the well. As they touched the water they became alive and began to swim around as though their ordeal had never happened.

In the church of St Neots, Cambridgeshire, is a stained glass window donated by the young men of the parish in 1528 that records the miracle of the fish.

It is said that the comb of St Neot was made of fish teeth, and had the appearance of a pike's jaw.

* * *

A STRANGE RECIPE FROM THE U.S.A.

Take a carp of around five pounds and lay it on an oak board of roughly the same size as the fish. Wrap both the carp and the board in burlap (sacking). Then soak in a marinade of Worcestershire sauce, vinegar, garlic, tomato juice, green peppers and crushed peppercorn. Soak for two days, remove from the marinade and smoke for a further two days over hickory chips, basting at regular intervals with remaining marinade. When the process is completed, unwrap the carp from the burlap. Then throw away the fish and eat the board.

* * *

An angler who caught a British record carp in 1995 caught it again in 2005 but, this time, had to pay £2,234 for it at auction.

The carp lived in a lake in Warmwell, Dorset for thirty-five years and was known as the Warmwell Whacker. It died in 1997 and was stuffed and mounted.

The angler from Gwent; Wales was determined to buy the fish when he heard it was going up for sale. He said, "It was a dream come true."

* * *

GOLDFISH

Although goldfish were bred in China for centuries they were unknown in Europe until about two hundred years ago when a few were given to Madame Pompadour of the court of King Louis XV of France. Madam Pompadour was the leader of fashion at the time and soon everybody who was somebody wanted a goldfish. Some other breeds were imported such as the fantail, the comet and the nymph. Now millions of people keep goldfish in ponds and aquariums. They are kept in hospitals, offices, restaurants and schools etc. and their slow, graceful swimming can be very therapeutic.

Status – Not Threatened

*
* IN *

2001 THE

ESTIMATED NUMBER

OF GOLDFISH KEPT AS PETS

IN THE UNITED

KINGDOM

WAS

14, 700, 000

WILLIAM THE GOLDFISH

For the love of William the goldfish, the R.S.P.C.A. local staff and eleven local residents of a street in Newcastle-Upon-Tyne, set up a rescue operation after William had been poured down a drain along with six of his pals. Unable to remove the drain grate, time was running out for William and his friends as they struggled for life in the filthy rubbish-strewn water. Eventually, William was freed but his six pals died. An R.S.P.C.A. inspector said: "William may only be a goldfish in the eyes of the person who poured him down the drain, but this street wanted him rescued."

William was found a new home in west Jesmond, Newcastle-Upon-Tyne.

* * *

A SICK FISH

Don't flush sick or badly injured fish down the loo; it can cause the fish to die a painful death as it struggles for air in the dark, stinking water of the sewer.

The most humane way, although not an easy way, is to wrap the sick fish in a damp piece of cloth and dash it with vigour onto a hard surface, i.e. a pathway or paving slab. This will kill the fish instantly and without pain. Again not an easy way but without pain.

GOD ASKED NOAH

God asked Noah to report to his office.

God: Noah, I want you to build me a new ark …Not just any ark though; I want it to be twenty stories high, and I want it full of fish … Not just any fish, I want it full of carp.

Noah: Let me get this straight; you want me to build you an ark twenty stories high and filled with carp?

God: That's correct.

Noah: So what you are saying is; you want me to build you a multi-story carp ark!

BOY

Not wanting the trouble of looking after an aquarium, a father tries to convince his young son that having a goldfish was not a good idea.

"The thing is, son," said the father., "we already have fish. There are two tins of tuna in the cupboard!"

* * *

GIRL

A little girl was distraught when her pet goldfish died. Her father suggested that they wrap up the dead fish in a piece of tissue and put it down the toilet.

"No! No!" cried the tearful little girl. "That's cruel."

"Then you tell me what to do with it, darling," said the sympathetic father.

The little girl thought for a moment and then said: "Let's give it to the cat to eat!"

* * *

PREGNANT LADY

A heavily pregnant lady gets on a bus carrying a goldfish in a bowl she had just bought from the pet shop. She asks the driver to go steady over the road humps because she is expecting to have her baby at any time; also, she does not want the water to slop around in the bowl and frighten the goldfish. Before reaching her stop the drivers change. The driver going off duty calls out to the driver coming on duty: "Go careful over the humps, Reg, there's a lady on board pregnant with a goldfish."

FAT CAT

A man was digging in his garden when his neighbour asked what he was doing.

"My goldfish died, I'm burying him," said the man.

"That's a big hole for a goldfish isn't it?" said the neighbour.

"That's because he's inside your cat," said the man.

* * *

T.V.

An aquarium of goldfish is an interactive feline T.V. When the cat is bored with watching the fish, they make a very good T.V. dinner.

* * *

WIGGLY GOLDFISH

Goldfish are slippery
Goldfish are wiggly
Some are quite serious
Some are quite giggly
Some swim in circles
And wave when they pass
Others make faces
And glare through the glass
Wiggly giggly
Most of all wet
You can't beat a goldfish
If you want a pet

Bidasara And The Golden Fish

Once upon a time in the city of Indrapoora, there lived a rich and prosperous merchant who had wealth beyond compare. But, the one thing he and his wife wanted most, they could not have – a child. One day as he and his wife were walking along a river bank they found an abandoned baby girl. They adopted the child and named her Bidasara. The merchant had a golden fish made and into the fish he transferred the soul of Bidasara. Then he put the fish into a golden box full of water and hid it in a pond in his garden.

In time, Bidasara grew to be a beautiful woman. Now the king of Indrapoora had a fair young queen who lived in fear that the king might take a second wife. Hearing of the charms of Bidasara, the queen resolved to put her out of the way. She lured Bidasara to the palace and tortured her cruelly. But Bidasara could not die because her soul was not in her. At last she could stand the torture no longer and said to the queen: "If you wish me to die, you must bring the golden box from my father's garden."

The queen had the box brought to her. Opening it she found the golden fish. Bidasara said: "My soul is in that fish. In the morning you must take the fish out of the water, and in the evening you must put it back. Don't let the fish lie about; but bind it around your neck. If you do this I shall soon die!"

So the queen took the golden fish and fastened it around her neck: No sooner had she done so than Bidasara fell into a swoon. But in the evening when the golden fish was placed back into the golden box, Bidasara came back to herself. Seeing that she had Bidasara in her power, the queen sent her home to her parents.

To save her from further persecution, her parents took her from the city and built a house in a lonely and isolated place and brought Bidasara there. There she lived alone.

All day long while the fish was out of water Bidasara remained unconscious. But in the evening, when the fish was put back into the water, she revived.

One day the king was out hunting and, coming to the isolated house he stopped to seek refreshment. Entering the house he found he unconscious Bidasara. He was overcome by her great beauty and tried to waken her; but in vain.

All during the next day, he could think of nothing but the beautiful sleeping girl. That evening, he returned to the house but still found her unconscious. He sat by her bed admiring her great beauty. Then, as darkness began to fall, Bidasara began to stir. She told the king all the secrets of her life.

The king became angry at the wickedness of his wife and on his return to the palace he took the golden fish from the queen and placed it back into the golden box. Immediately, Bidasara revived.

The king banished the queen from his kingdom and took Bidasara for his wife. And as a token of his love for her, the king gave Bidasara the golden box in which was the golden fish in which was her soul.

NONSENSE TALES

Where Was Its Body?

Two fisherman were arguing about which one of them came from the best village. One fisherman boasted that once a fisherman in his village had caught a fish that was so big that if you stood it on its tail its head would reach the sky.

The second fisherman smiled and said that in his village a fisherman had caught a fish so big that its top lip touched the sky and its bottom lip touched the ground.

"So where was its body?" asked the first fisherman.

"No one knows,' said the second fisherman, 'it was only ever seen with its mouth open."

*

A Dark and Stormy Night

It was a dark and stormy night, and all the fisherman were gathered in the galley. The skipper turned to the first mate and said, "Tell us a story."

The first mate began; "It was a dark and stormy night, and all the fisherman were gathered in the galley. The skipper turned to the first mate and said, 'Tell us a story.' The first mate began; 'It was a dark and stormy night…'"

Oh, The Brave Fisher's Life

John Chalkhill
1600-1642

Oh, the brave fisher's life,
It is the best of any,
'tis full of pleasure, void of strife,
And 'tis beloved of many;
Other joys
Are but toys,
Only this
Lawful is,
For our skill
Breeds no ill,
But content and pleasure.

In the morning up we rise
Ere aurora's peeping,
Drink a cup to wash our eyes,
Leave the sluggard sleeping;
Then we go
To and fro,
With our knacks
At our backs,
To such streams
As the Thames,
If we have the leisure.

When we please to walk abroad
For our recreation,
In the fields is our abode
Full of delectation:
Where in a brook
With a hook,
Or a lake
Fish we take,
There we sit
For a bit, till the fish entangle.

We have gentles in the horn,
We have paste and worms too,
We can watch both night and morn,
Suffer rain and storms too:
None do here
Use to swear,
Oaths do fray
Fish away,
We sit still,
Watch our quill,
Fishers must not wrangle.

If the sun's excessive heat
Makes our bodies swelter,
To an osier hedge we get
For a friendly shelter,
Where in a dike
Perch or pike,
Roach or dace
We do chase,
Bleak or gudgeon,
Without grudging,
We are still contented.

Or we sometimes pass an hour
Under a green willow,
That defends us from a show'r,
Making earth our pillow;
There we may
Think and pray
Before death
Stops our breath:
Other joys
Are but toys
And to be lamented.

HAI HO SHANG

The Hai Ho Shang was believed to be the most fearsome of all sea beasts by Chinese fishermen who believed that this evil fish would drag them and their boats to their doom beneath the waves.

To ward off the Hai Ho Shang, fishermen would carry a bag of feathers with them when they set sail. They believed that the monster fish could not stand the smell of burning feathers. If a Hai Ho Shang was sighted a fisherman who was trained in the steps of a special dance would perform the dance while burning the feathers. If done correctly the Hai Ho Shang would become peaceful and placid and leave the fishermen to cast their nets in peace.

When young Hai Ho Shang were caught in their nets they would raise up their fins as if begging the fishermen to spare their lives. But the fishermen were so afraid of them growing to full size they killed them all. Until recently, Chinese fishermen would traditionally carry a bag of feathers on board their boats when setting out to their fishing grounds.

* * *

MAKAKA

The makaka appears in the Hindu religion a sea creature with the body of an animal and the tail of a fish. The most well known makaka in the Hindu faith is one that has the head of an elephant and the tail of a fish. The Hindu believe that the goddess Ganga rode on the back of the makaka down the holy river of India spreading good luck, wisdom and wealth to all who came to bathe in her river.

Another makaka has the tail of a fish and the head and legs of a goat and is believed to represent the goat fish Capricorn – the tenth sign of the zodiac. So long as it has the tail of a fish, the makaka can have the head and body of any mammal.

PUFFERFISH
Diodon Maculatas

The pufferfish is the most poisonous fish in the world. It can deliver a fatal toxin called tetrodotoxin. Less than 0.1g (0.0004 oz) can kill an adult person in less than twenty minutes. Known in Japan as fugu-sashi, it is served as a delicacy by specially licensed chefs. Even so, despite stringent safeguards, severe illness and death still occur when fugu-sashi has been prepared incorrectly. Between thirty and a hundred people are poisoned each year through eating ill-prepared fugu-sashi.

Status − Vunerable

BLUEFIN TUNA
Thunnus Thynnus

In 1991 in Tokyo, a giant Bluefin Tuna was turned into over 2,400 servings of sushi, with each diner paying forty-five pounds per serving. It was estimated that the takings from this giant fish was a staggering one hundred and eight thousand, four hundred and thirty-three pounds!

Status − Northern Bluefin Tuna − Threatened
Southern Bluefin Tuna − Critically Endangered

A northern bluefin tuna weighing 600-660lb (270-300kg) can produce ten million eggs in a single spawning. When we eat tuna with our salad we become the ultimate consumer in a long food chain. The tuna would have fed on cod and mackerel who, in their turn, would have fed on herring and other small fish. Herring feed off tiny crustaceans who, in their turn, feed off microscopic plants called plankton. Biologists estimate that each step in the food chain takes as much as five tons of plankton to make a single pound of tuna.

THE GRAVEYARD

In the graveyard of Ripon Cathederal, North Yorkshire is a
gravestone that bears this epitaph:

Here lies poor, but honest
Brian Tunstall
He was a most expert angler.
Until death, envious of his merit;
threw out his line, hooked him and landed him here
the 21st day of April 1790.

* * *

EPITAPH OF AN ANGLER

*
* He *
Angled
Many A
Purling Brook
but lacked the
Angler's skill
he lied a-
bout the
fish he
Took
And
Here
He's lying still

MYRTLE THE HADDOCK

A skinny old haddock named myrtle
Was once seduced by a turtle;
The result of this mate
Was five plaice and a skate
Proving the turtle was fertile

* * *

THE MERMAIDS THAT SING

How often and often I wish
I could live the blue sea like a fish!
Not a sound, not a thing,
But the mermaids that sing,
Whilst their tails give a silvery swish

* * *

TWO CATFISH OF ABERGAVENNY

Two catfish of Abergavenny,
Each thought there was one catfish to many,
So they snarled and they spit
They scratched and they bit,
Till barring their nails
At the end of their tails,
Instead of two catfish there weren't any.

PIRANHA

Pygocentrus Rooseveltiella

"They are the most ferocious fish in the world. They will rend and devour alive any wounded man or beast; for blood in the water excites them to madness. The head, with its short muzzle, staring malignant eyes and gaping cruelly armed jaws, is the embodiment of evil ferocity."

Theodore Roosevelt
(1858-1919)

*

Horror stories abound about this savage, bloodthirsty marauder.

It was reported that as many as three hundred people were devoured by a shoal of piranhas when their boat sank near Obides, Brazil in 1981. And a group of starving prospectors dynamited a stream to obtain food after seeing a shoal of piranhas. Wading in to pick up the dead fish, one starving man put one straight into his mouth. The fish was not dead and bit such a large chunk from his tongue that his companions were only just able to save him from bleeding to death.

*

Amazon Indians use the teeth of the piranha to make knives and scissors.

Status – Not Threatened

ANGLING CLUB

The local angling club were furious when they found someone had decided to dump his five pet piranhas in their fishing lake. A bailiff reported back to the committee that he had seen just one piranha gobble up four prime fish in one twentieth of an hour.

The chairman gasps. "That means all five could empty the lake in just one hour."

How many fish was the lake stocked with?

Answer on page 151

The Miracle of the Fish and the Ring

Nest was the beautiful wife of Mealgwn Gwynedd king of north Wales. The king loved Nest dearly and to prove his love he gave her a precious ring that could only be worn by the queens of north Wales.

One day while bathing in a pool, the ring slipped from her finger. Nest was panic stricken and dived to the bottom of the pool in search of the precious ring. Unable to find it she was overcome with grief and guilt and was afraid to tell the king.

Nest sought the help of St Asaph, who, it was said to have shone with 'virtue and miracles from the flower of his earliest youth.' After hearing Nest's story, the saint invited the royal couple to dine with him the following evening. When Mealgwn and Nest arrived St Asaph told the king how Nest had lost the ring. The king was furious and refused to believe her story.

The saint invited the king and queen to pray with him that the ring might be found. After prayers, the three of them sat down to eat. They started the meal with fish that had been caught in the river Elwy that same day. As the king cut open his fish the precious ring of the queens of north Wales fell out onto his plate.

The Fisher Lass
Wallace Irwin
1875-1959

When I was young and full o'pride
A standing on the grass
And gazin' o'er the waterside
I seen a fisher lass.
"O fisher lass, be kind a while,"
I ask her quite unbid,
"Please look into me face and smile,"
And blow me eyes she did!
"Blow me light, and blow me blow
I didn't think she'd charm me so
But blow me eyes she did!

* * *

Upon the River Bank Serene

Upon the river bank serene
A fisher stood while all was green
And looked it.

He saw just as the light grew dim
A fish – or the fish saw him
And hooked it.

He took with high elected-comb
The fish – or else the story – home
And cooked it.

Recording angels by his bed
Weighed all that he had said
And booked it.

SHARK!

Of the two hundred and fifty species of shark, twenty-five are classified as dangerous to man. The largest of these is the world's largest flesh-eating fish, the Great White, (carcharodon carcharias) which grows up to twenty-one feet (6.4cm) long. There have been unverified reports of great whites reaching thirty-seven feet (11.3m). Although the great white has a fearsome reputation, the shark most dangerous to man is the tiger shark (galaocerdo curvier). Proportionately more tiger shark attacks are fatal to man than attacks from the great whites.

Status – Great White: Not Threatened
            Tiger Shark: Threatened

*

Sharks are covered in special scales called denticles. These are like tiny hooks that are embedded in the skin and pointed backwards making the shark's skin extremely abrasive. They also make the skin extremely hard wearing, so much so, that jackets, belts and even shoes can be made from this tough and highly durable skin. Fishermen once used the rough, scaly skin of the shark to scrub the decks of their ships.

*

Sharks have incredibly sensitive noses for hunting down their prey, but have two other deadly senses: they have acute hearing that can pick up the frequency pulses given off by an injured fish, and tiny clusters of cells under their skins allow them to feel the tiniest electrical impulses given out by all creatures.

World Wild Life Fund

In 1994 the World Wild Life Fund estimated that the number of sharks killed was between 40 and 70 million each year. A great many of them "finned". That is, the fins are cut off and the still living creature thrown back into the sea, where, unable to swim, they slowly drown. In 1998 you could buy a kilo of shark's fins for a hundred and ten dollars and a bowl of shark fin soup would cost about a hundred dollars.

* * *

Statistics
show that you
are
more likely to
be
attacked by a
cow
than a shark.

WHALE SHARK

Rhiniodon Typus

The whale shark is the biggest fish in the world and can grow up to fifty feet long (15m). This gentle giant feeds on plankton, which it filters through its gills as it swims. A timid animal, it will shy away from noise created by scuba divers. 'Riding' the whale shark interferes with its natural behaviour and should be discouraged.

Status – Vunerable

DWARF LANTERN FISH

Etmopterus perryi

The smallest sharks are the dwarf lantern fish. Fully grown females grow to about eight inches (20cm) and seven inches for males (18cm)

Status – Data Deficient

CARCHAROCLES MEGALODON

The megalodon may have been the largest predator to have ever lived. Its full size is debated, but lengths of 15 to 20 metres are widely accepted which means that megalodon was at least three times as big as the great white. Megalodon became extinct about two million years ago. This fearsome shark had teeth the size of a person's hand!

Status – Extinct

THE ROMAN GALLEY

A Roman galley was sailing back to Rome with a cargo of Christian slaves. Two Roman slave masters standing on deck see a massive man-eating shark swimming in the wake of the ship. Thinking they could have a little fun, they throw one of the slaves overboard. The slave starts to swim for his life but soon realises he has no chance of out-swimming the shark. He stops swimming and raises his hand to the sky. "Lord," he prays, "please turn this fearsome shark into a Christian." Instantly, the shark stops swimming, closes its eyes, puts its massive fins together and says: "For what we are about to receive…"

A shark fisherman gets pulled overboard
after hooking a monster shark.
Trying to keep calm in the water,
he starts to pray:
"O Lord, if you cannot help me
please don't help that shark!"

126

MISS WATSON

Then, Miss Watson, she took me in the closet and prayed, but nothing came of it. She told me to pray every day and whatever I asked for I would get it.

Once, I got a fish-line but no hooks. It waren't any good to me without hooks. I tried for hooks three or four times but somehow I couldn't make it work.

I ask Miss Watson to try for me but she said I was a fool. She never told me why and I couldn't make it out no way.

Tom Sawyer

Don't tell fish stories
where the people know you;
But particularly,
don't tell them where
they know the fish.

Mark Twain

SINARPAN GOBY

Mistichthys Luzonen

It would take 70,000 of these tiny fish to make a one pound fishcake. They measure just 1.3cm.

Status – Fifty-eight members of the Goby family
are threatened while five family members
are critically endangered.

* * *

SEA HEDGEHOG

Diodon Maclatus

The sea hedgehog of South America is less than a foot long; yet this little fish can kill a twenty-five foot long shark! When swallowed by a shark it puffs itself up and projects spines in all directions from its body. Then it calmly starts eating its way out causing the shark to die a slow lingering death.

Status – Data Deficient

* * *

The Fisher Lad Of Whitby

Unknown

My love he was a fisher-lad, and when he came ashore
He always steer'd to me, to greet me at the door;
For he knew I loved him well, as anyone could see,
And O but I was fain when he came a courting me.

It was one lovely morning, one morning in May,
He took me in his boat to sail out on the bay;
Then he told me of his love, as he sat by my side,
And he said that in a month he would make me his bride.

That very afternoon a man of war came in the bay;
And the press-gang came along and took my fisher-lad
away;
Put irons on his hands, and irons on his feet,
And they carried him aboard, to fight in the fleet.

My father often talks of the perils of the main,
And my mother says she hopes he will come back again;
But I know he never will; for in my dreams I see
His body lying low at the bottom of the sea.

The ships come sailing in, and the ships they sail away,
And the sailors sing their merry songs out on the bay;
But for me my heart is breaking, and I only wish to be,
Lying low with my fisher-lad deep down in the sea.

When the house is all still, and everyone asleep,
I sit upon my bed, and bitterly I weep;
And I think of my fisher-lad away down in the deep.
For he never, never more, will come again to me.

MUSICAL FISH

Salmon Chanted Evening
Bass In Street Blues
You Don't Send Me Flounders Any More
Prawn In The U.S.A.
My Carp Will Go On
It's A Long Way To Kipperary
When You Fish Upon A Star
Day Bream Believer
A Hard Dace Night
Mr Sandman Bring Me A Bream
That's A Moray
Clam Every Mountain
Shark! The Herald Angels Sing
The Impossible Bream
I Wish I Could Shimmy Like My Sister Skate
The First Time Ever I Saw Your Dace
Shrimply The Best

THE CRAB FISH

English folk song

It's of a jolly clergyman he had a little horse
A bridle and a saddle, to cock his leg across

And as he was a-riding, a-riding by a brook
He saw a little man with a fishing rod and hook

'O fisherman, O fisherman, O fisherman,' said he
'Have you got a little crab-fish that you will sell to me?'

'O yes sir, O yes sir, O yes sir,' said he
'The finest in the basket I will sell to thee!'

So he took the little crab-fish, he took him by the horns
He slung him on his back and toddles him off home

But when he got it home, boys, he couldn't find a dish
So he popped it in a pot, boys, that wasn't used for fish

And when his wife got out of bed in the middle of the night
The naughty little crab-fish gave her such a bite

She shouted to her husband and quickly he arose
And the naughty little crab-fish it caught him by the nose

It's: 'Husband, O husband, as sure as I was born
The devil's in the Charlie, a sticking up his horn'

'Wife, wife, wife, you must be going mad
That you don't know the devil from an old sea crab'

Then one got a stick and the t'other got a broom
And they chased that poor old crab-fish all round the room

They kicked him on the head; they kicked him on the side
They jumped upon his back, boys, until the poor crab died

THE CRANE AND THE WISE CRAB

A crane grew too old and feeble to catch the fish that lived in a lake close to his nest. So, after thinking the matter over, he resolved to do by cunning what he could no longer do by force, and he said to a crab in the lake:

'My dear friend, whatever will you and all the fishes do now? Some men are coming soon to drain the water from the lake. You will all be caught and killed!'

On hearing this terrible news all the fishes assembled to try to find some way of escape. 'I have thought of a plan,' said the cunning old crane. Of course I eat one or two of you now and then; but I don't want you to perish in a heap for want of water. What good would that do me? Now, there is a large pond just a few hundred yards away. Let me carry you, one by one, in my beak to this safe place.'

The fish got an old carp to go with the crane and see if there was such pond. The crane took him very gently in his beak and showed him the new stretch of water, and then put him back among his companions. When the fishes heard about the pond they cried, 'Very well, Mr Crane; you can take us all with you!' The cunning old crane meant to take the fishes one by one in his beak, and eat them under a tree far away from the pond; but, unhappily for him, he began with the wise crab.

'Come along,' he said to the crab, 'and let me take you in my beak to the new pond.'

'I don't like to trust myself in your beak,' said the crab. 'You might let me fall and break my shell. We crabs have a famous grip. Let me catch hold of you round the neck, and then you can take me.'

The crane did not see that the crab was trying to out wit him, and agreed to the proposal. But when the crab was fixed on his neck, instead of going to the pond, he went to the tree.

'Where is the pond?' said the crab. 'Pond?' said the wicked old crane.

'Do you think I'm taking all this trouble for nothing? The whole thing is just a trick for catching you and the other fishes, one by one, and eating you.'

'Just as I thought,' said the crab. And he drove his claws into the neck of the wicked old crane, and killed him.

THE CRAB AND THE COW

In the beginning all the animals on earth spoke just the same as men. But they were always betraying the secrets of heaven, which annoyed the gods, who punished them with dumbness.

In those days the crab was round and smooth. One day a cow was secretly eating rice in a field when a red crab saw it and began to shout, 'The cow is stealing rice!'

The cow crossly told the crab to mind its own business, but the crab took no notice and merely shouted louder. This so enraged the cow that she lifted up her foot and stamped on the crab.

The poor crab was squashed flat, and you can still see the mark of the cows hoof on the shells of crabs.

IDIOMS

THE GREAT FISHER OF SOULS
Satan

*

A FISHER OF MEN
A saver of souls

*

FISHING FOR COMPLIMENTS
To seek praise

*

SMELLS FISHY
Not quite as it should be

*

DRINK LIKE A FISH
To drink alcohol in excess

*

A BIG FISH IN A SMALL POND
Important within a limited scope

*

SLEEPING WITH THE FISHES
Murder victim dumped at sea

*

A DULL FISH
Of little emotion

IDIOMS

FEED TO THE FISHES
Kill by drowning

*

BIG FISH
An important or influential person

*

LOOSE FISH
One of careless manner

*

TO MAKE FISH OF ONE, FLESH OF THE OTHER
To discriminate unfairly

*

A MIRACLE ON THE SCALE OF LOAVES AND
FISHES
To do the impossible

*

TO FISH IN TROUBLED WATERS
To profit out of upheaval

*

I WOULDN'T WALK YOU AROUND THE HERRING
BARREL
A contemptuous rejection

*

A QUEER FISH
An eccentric person

IDIOMS

OTHER FISH TO FRY
Other things to attend to

*

FISH OUT OF WATER
To be in an unwelcome situation

*

LIKE SHOOTING FISH IN A BARREL
So easy as to be unfair

*

TO SKIN AN EEL BY THE TAIL
To do things the wrong way

*

LOSE IN HAKE GAIN IN HERRING
Lose one way but gain in another

*

ALL THE FISH THAT COME INTO MY NET
To deal in anything to make a profit

*

NOR FISH, FLESH, OR GOOD RED HERRING
Not fit for one thing or another

*

A FINE MORNING TO CATCH HERRING ON
NEWMARKET HEATH
Rainy weather

THE HUNGRY FOX

A hungry fox saw a fine fat fish swimming in a shallow stream and decided he would make a meal of it. Just as he was about to spring on the fish he heard a loud noise. Looking up, he saw a drum hanging in a tree, and as the wind blew, the branches beat upon the drum.

'Ah! Ah!' said the fox. 'A thing that can make so much noise must certainly have more flesh on it than that fat fish'

So, allowing the fish to swim away, he sprang upon the drum; but when he tore the drum apart he found that there was nothing whatsoever inside.

'What a fool I am!' said the fox. 'I have missed a fine fish meal for nothing.'

Moral:

By being greedy we may miss something that is worth having.

*

THE WISE FISH

Three fishes lived in a stream. The first fish was wise, the second had a little sense, and the third had no sense at all. A fisherman saw the three fishes, and went to get his net.

'I must get out of this stream at once,' said the wise fish. And he threw himself into a little channel that led to a river.

The other two fishes did not try to escape at all.

Soon the fisherman returned with his nets, and blocked up the channel leading to the river. The second fish wished he had followed the wise fish, but he soon thought of a plan to escape. He floated upside down on the surface of the water, and the fisherman, thinking he was dead, did not bother with him.

But the foolish fish was caught by the fisherman, who had him for his supper.

Moral: We should all endeavour to be wise

DEAN SWIFT

Dean Swift, benighted at an Irish monastery; breakfasting next morning – a Friday – on bacon and eggs. But the monks, of course, were having fish. A display of Irish wit followed, the monks leading off with grace:

> "From bacon and eggs
> and rotten legs"
> (Swift was poor on his feet)
> "good Lord deliver us!"

Swift immediately countered with:

> "From oysters and cockles
> and men without bottles,
> good Lord deliver us."

He followed this up with the lines:
Does any man of common sense
Think ham and eggs give God offence?
Or that a herring has charm
The Almighty's anger to disarm?
Wrapped in His majesty divine,
D'you think he cares on what we dine?

*

THE CHIP MONK

One day while driving home from a fishing trip in the pouring rain, a man got a flat tyre outside a monastery. A monk came out and invited him inside to have dinner and spend the night. The motorist accepted and that night had a wonderful dinner of fish and chips. He decided to compliment the chef. Entering the kitchen he asked the cook:

"Are you the fish frier?"

"No," replied the cook. "I'm the chip monk."

138

DIE LAUGHING

A doctor in Denmark laughed so much when watching the movie *A Fish Called Wanda*, his heartbeat went from the normal sixty beats a minute to almost five hundred beats a minute. He had a heart attack and died.

Proof that you can die laughing!

* * *

KILLING THE FISH

We're fishing and my wife had a problem killing the fish. I wasn't crazy with that part either. But I figured if we just waited for the fish to die naturally it could take forever; certainly 'till after supper.

Paul Reiser

THREE JOLLY FISHERMEN

Folk song

There were three jolly fishermen,
There were three jolly fishermen,
Fisher, fisher, men, men, men.
Fisher, fisher, men, men, men.
There were three jolly fishermen.

The first fisherman's name was Abraham.
The first fisherman's name was Abraham.
Abra, abra, ham, ham, ham.
Abra, abra, ham, ham, ham.
The first fisherman's name was Abraham.

The next fisherman's name was Isaac
The next fisherman's name was Isaac
I, I, saac, saac, saac.
I, I, saac, saac, saacc.
The next fisherman name was Isaac.

The third fisherman's name was Jacob.
The third fisherman's name was Jacob
Jay, jay, cob, cob, cob.
Jay, jay, cob, cob, cob.
The third fisherman's name was Jacob.

They all fished up in Jericho.
They all fished up in Jericho,
Jerry, Jerry, co, co, co.
Jerry, Jerry, co, co, co.
They all fished up in Jericho.

They should have fished in Amsterdam,.
They should have fished in Amsterdam.
Amster, Amster, sh, sh, sh.
Amster, Amster, sh, sh, sh.
Mustn't say that naughty word.

I think I'll say it anyway.
I think I'll say it anyway.
Any, any, way, way, way.
Any, any, way, way, way.
I think I'll say it anyway.

They should have fished in Amsterdam.
They should have fished in Amsterdam.
Amster, Amster, dam, dam, dam.
Amster, Amster, dam, dam, dam.
They should have fished in Amsterdam,

A FISHERMAN

A fisherman had good day fishing on a local trout stream and on his way home he decided to stop off at the pub to have a well-earned pint.

After setting his pint down on the bar, the landlord asks how he had got on.

'Well,' said the fisherman, 'there were twice-four and twenty trout swimming in the rain.

'I caught and killed a seventh part, so how many did remain?'

Answer on page 151

THE LITTLE FISH

Jane and Ann Taylor
1783-1842   1782-1866

'Dear Mother,' said the little fish,
'Is that not a little fly?
I'm very hungry, and I wish
You'd let me go and try'.

'Sweet innocent,' the mother cried
And started from her nook,
'That horrible fly is put to hide
The sharpness of the hook.'

Now, as I've heard, this little trout
Was young and foolish too,
And so he thought he'd venture out,
To see if it was true.

And round about the hook he played
With many a longing look,
 And – 'Dear me', to himself he said,
'I'm sure that's not a hook.'

'I can but give one little pluck:
Let's see and so I will.'
So on he went, and lo! It stuck
Quite through his little gill.

And as he faint and fainter grew,
With hollow voice he cried,
'Dear mother, had I minded you
 I need not now have died.'

The Wreck Of The Howe

Alfred Hutchinson
'Hurricane Hutch'
Circa 1931

One night on the rocks off Bear Island
A trawler named the *Howe* ran ashore,
Right on those cursed hidden 'blinders',*
To remain there a wreck evermore.
No tugs in the world could have saved her
But one went his luck to try
And found her a wreck that was hopeless,
To leave her there, high and dry.

Her skipper was a man named McGregor,
As brave as the brave known to be,
He said: 'Now she's a wreck, boys, for ever,
But you'll take your orders from me.
Your lives all depend on good discipline,
So be cheerful and keep a big heart.
For the sake of your wives and your families
Each of you must play your part.'

But out in that dark arctic region
Just imagine the dire plight of the crew,
With their ship on the rocks of Bear island
There was nothing on earth they could do.
Their 'sparks' was a brave lad of twenty,
His message for help he had sent.
Thank God it was answered by plenty,
And bravely to her aid they went.

They found her a wreck at the mercy
Of a sea that no pen can describe.
They couldn't get anywhere near her
Yet time out of number they tried.
On the deck they could see the poor fellows standing,
And who would deny they were brave,
Facing their deaths, calm and steadfast
On the brink of a sailor's grave.

So round to the lee of the island,
Each vessel sent picked men ashore
To battle across land that was barren
And untrodden by human foot before.
And god only knows what hardships,
They faced on that bleak winter night,
Hands, faces, feet were frost-bitten
But they struggled on without sup or bite.

On the *Howe*, to that brave seaman, Harper,
A rope round his body they tied,
To swim to a point that meant rescue.
He failed, but I praise him, he tried.
He was pulled back on board by his comrades,
And there on the wreck he lay 'beat',
But a hero, if ever there was one,
The whitest of men you could meet.

Still high on those rocks up above them,
With courage, those men struggled on,
Till they found them, and brought off the rescue,
They saved the whole crew, every one.
Those lads were brought back to Grimsby,
And to see them again – it was grand!
We know not one half what they suffered,
But we kid them that we understand.

We thank you, brave men, for that rescue,
Your deed was truly gallant – well done!
It may not have gone down to history,
It is even forgotten by some.
But I myself, a fisherman,
Will remember to my dying day,
And no gold in the world could repay you,
Had they called it a job for pay.

And a word for you that were rescued,
For some of you are well known to me.
No words could I write that could praise you enough,
For your conduct, so gallant at sea.
You held up that fine British tradition,
You sent up its prestige, sky high,
Those grim nights on the rocks at bear island,
Where in silence you were prepared to die.

Well, that is the life of the fisher
As told in this tale of the sea,
Lives are so often the price
Of that fish you have eaten for tea.
But seldom you'll hear these men grumble,
It's come day, or go day with them.
Just trusting to God in his mercy,
And thank him for that – Amen!

* The Howe hit a 'blinder' (submerged rock)
on the 19th November 1931.

146

THE FISHERMEN FROM
HULL AND GRMBSY

In memory of the fishermen from
Hull and Grimsby who lost their lives
in the gale of 8 and 9 February 1889.

Methinks I see some little crafts spreading their sails al-lee
As down the Humber they did glide bound for the northern sea,
Methinks I see on each small craft a crew with hearts so brave,
Going to earn their daily bread upon the restless wave.

Methinks I see them as they left the land all far behind,
Casting the lead into the deep their fishing grounds to find;
Methinks I see them on the deck working with a will,
To shoot their nets into the deep either for good or ill.

Methinks I see them shoot their trawl upon a Thursday night,
And saw the watch upon the deck, and everything was right;
Methinks I see them yet again when daylight did appear,
All hands working with a will getting off their gear.

Methinks I see the net on board and fish so fresh and gay,
And all were busily engaged clearing them away;
Methinks I see them pull away into the ice below,
And then the sea began to rise, and the wind did stronger blow.

Methinks I heard the skipper say, 'my lads, we'll shorten sail,
As the sky to all appearance looks like an approaching gale';
Methinks I see them yet again, and all on board was right,
With sails close reef'd, the deck cleared up, and side lights
burning bright

Methinks I see them yet again, the midnight hour was passed,
Their little craft was battling there with the fiery blast;
Methinks I heard the skipper say, 'cheer up, my lads, be brave,
We'll trust in him who rules the deep, in him who alone can save.'

Methinks I read the thought of them who now are called away,
They were thinking of their loved ones dear and many miles away;
Thinking of wife and children dear, and aged parents too
Who no more will see them here again in this world below.

Great god, thou sees each sorrowing heart, the widow in distress,
Thou knows the little children dear, who now are fatherless;
Comfort and cheer them here below, and lead them by thy hand,
And at last may meet their loved ones dear in the Promised Land.

Every year twenty-five offshore fishermen lose
their lives at sea around the coast of Britain.

THE SEAFARERS HYMN
William Whiting
1825-1878

Eternal Father, strong to save,
Whose arm hath bound the restless wave,
Who bidst the mighty ocean deep
Its own appointed limits keep;
O, hear us when we cry to thee
For those in peril on the sea!

O, Christ, whose voice the waters heard,
And hushed their raging at thy word,
Who walkedst on the foaming deep,
And calm amid the storm didst sleep;
O, hear us when we cry to thee
For those in peril on the sea!

O Holy Spirit, who didst brood
Upon the chaos dark and rude,
And bid its angry tumult cease,
And give, for wild confusion, peace;
O, hear us when we cry to thee
For those in peril on the sea!

O trinity of love and power,
Our brethren shield in dangers hour:
From rock and tempest, fire and foe,
Protect them wheresoe'er they go:
Thus evermore shall rise to thee
Glad hymns of praise from land and sea.

ANSWERS

COD – NUNDRUMS

Page 12
It's not the size of your rod that counts it's how you use it.

*

Men are like fish, neither would get into trouble
if they kept their mouths shut

Page 60
Resolutions are like eels, easy to catch but hard to hang on
to.

Page 61
An oyster is a fish built like a nut.

*

The gods do not deduct from man's alloted span
the hours spent fishing.

Page 71
Life is something you do when you can't go fishing.

*

Living would be much easier if men showed as much
patience at home as they do when they're fishing.

Page 85
Old fisherman never die they just smell that way.

*

Never fish for compliments, you never really catch
anything.

PUZZLE ANSWERS

The Canoeist

Page 56

Every three strokes the canoeist paddled, the edge of the circle moved one stroke from the point of the salmons leap. So after twelve strokes of paddling, the edge of the circle had moved out four strokes. Therefor the salmon jumped sixteen strokes away from the canoe.

*

The Old Lady

Page 86

She bought twelve pieces of cod and eight pieces of haddock

*

The Angling Club

Page 120

Four hundred fish

*

The Fisherman

Page 142

Four salmon remained.
Altogether there were 28 salmon
(twice-four equals 8 plus 20)
and as the fisherman caught a seventh part
that means he caught four.
As the other salmon had swum away,
fthe four he caught were the ones that remained.

151

CURIOUS

The curious thing about fishing is you never

           want to go home. If you catch anything, you

can't stop. If you don't catch anything, you hate

           to leave in case something might bite.

~ FIN ~